POLICY APPROACHES TO SUPPORT GREEN FINANCING OF MICRO, SMALL, AND MEDIUM-SIZED ENTERPRISES

ASIA-PACIFIC FINANCIAL INCLUSION FORUM

DECEMBER 2025

ASIAN DEVELOPMENT BANK

6 ADB Avenue, Mandaluyong City, 1550 Metro Manila, Philippines
Tel +63 2 8632 4444; Fax +63 2 8636 2444
www.adb.org

ISBN 978-92-9277-579-7 (print); 978-92-9277-580-3 (PDF); 978-92-9277-581-0 (ebook)
Publication Stock No. TCS250535-2
DOI: http://dx.doi.org/10.22617/TCS250535-2

Notes:
In this publication, "$" refers to United States dollars.
ADB recognizes "China" as the People's Republic of China and "Hong Kong" as Hong Kong, China.

Cover design by Michael Cortes.

Contents

Table, Figures, and Boxes

Table

Figures

Boxes

Acknowledgments

The Asia-Pacific Financial Inclusion Forum (APFIF) is a policy initiative established in 2010 under the Asia-Pacific Economic Cooperation (APEC) Finance Ministers' Process, housed within the APEC Business Advisory Council. The Asian Development Bank (ADB) leads the forum in collaboration with the Asian Development Bank Institute (ADBI) and implementation support provided by the Griffith Asia Institute.

The APFIF 2023–2024 report was prepared by the Regional Cooperation and Integration Division (ERCI) of ADB's Economic Research and Development Impact Department. Development of the report was aided by technical assistance TA 9922: Strengthening Regional Cooperation and Knowledge Sharing on the Application of Technology in Financial Services, financed by ADB's Technical Assistance Special Fund (TASF). Production was supported by TA 6592: Building Financial Resilience and Stability to Reinvigorate Growth. This was financed by the Investment Climate Facilitation Fund under the Regional Cooperation and Integration Financing Partnership Facility, the People's Republic of China Poverty Reduction and Regional Cooperation Fund, the Republic of Korea e-Asia and Knowledge Partnership Fund, and ADB's TASF.

The report benefited greatly from discussions at the 13th and 14th annual APFIF policy dialogues on 21–22 June 2023 in Tokyo, Japan and 30 May 2024 in Cusco, Peru. These events were attended by senior government officials, policy experts, and industry leaders from multiple economies across Asia and the Pacific and Latin America. The report summarizes proposed actions developed for APEC policymakers and regulators through these dialogues.

Under overall guidance by ERCI Director Jong Woo Kang, the preparation of the report was led by Rolando Avendano (economist, ERCI, ADB) and Paulo Rodelio Halili (principal economics officer, ERCI, ADB), with administrative support provided by Amiel Bryan Esperanza (operations assistant, ERCI, ADB). The main authors of the report are Shawn Hunter (adjunct research fellow, Griffith Asia Institute and consultant, ADB); Robert Bianchi (professor of finance and director of the Griffith Centre for Personal Finance and Superannuation, Griffith University); Ivan Diaz-Rainey (professor of finance, Griffith University); Xuan Ngo (PhD candidate, Griffith University); Akihiro Omura (senior lecturer of finance, Department of Accounting, Finance and Economics, Griffith University); and Victor Wong (senior lecturer of finance, Department of Accounting, Finance and Economics, Griffith University); Rolando Avendano (economist, ERCI, ADB); and Paulo Rodelio Halili (principal economics officer, ERCI, ADB).

Comments from Peter Morgan (former senior consulting economist and advisor to the dean, ADBI) are gratefully acknowledged.

Two shorter versions of this report were submitted to APEC Finance Ministers as part of the recommendations by APEC Business Advisory Council (ABAC) in August 2023 and in October 2024.

Eric Van Zant edited the manuscript, Michael Cortes created the cover design and implemented the typesetting and layout. Lawrence Casiraya proofread the publication, with assistance from Carol Ongchangco. The Printing Services Unit of ADB's Corporate Services Department and the Publishing Team of the Department of Communications and Knowledge Management supported printing and publishing.

Executive Summary

Access to green finance is one of the main challenges faced by firms today and a key pillar in the transition to a less carbon-intensive economy. In the case of micro, small, and medium-sized enterprises (MSMEs), it is crucially important. Among many Asia-Pacific Economic Cooperation (APEC) members, MSMEs are important contributors to gross domestic product (GDP) and employment. Yet, many small businesses still face serious obstacles in readily tapping into green finance and implementing initiatives. Ensuring such access is therefore essential for these businesses to address environmental challenges and integrate in global supply chains.

This report by the Asian Development Bank, in collaboration with the Asian Development Bank Institute and partners in the Asia-Pacific Financial Inclusion Forum, aims to examine the role of green finance for MSMEs, the policy actions undertaken by APEC members, and the channels by which MSMEs can access these new types of financing opportunities.

The Asia-Pacific Financial Inclusion Forum is a policy initiative of the APEC Finance Ministers' Process. It was proposed by the APEC Business Advisory Council to identify actions that policymakers and regulators can implement to put financial services within reach of the underserved.

What Is Green Finance?

Definitions of green finance vary widely. From a broad perspective, however, green finance can best be defined as any financial activity which ensures a better environmental outcome. For government agencies, green finance is critical for all economies, as it is under its various frameworks that authorities can deliver both economic growth and stronger environmental outcomes. Green finance also provides governments with a tool to achieve their United Nations Sustainable Development Goal targets for a cleaner economic future.

The Importance of Green Finance to MSMEs

It is worth reiterating that the transformation of APEC members to greener economies relies on MSMEs, as they represent a significant component of GDP, and thus need access to green instruments if this green transition is to occur. Green finance needs to be developed to ensure these solutions are available to this important economic segment. Green finance includes such instruments as green bonds, renewable energy financing, energy-efficient loans, carbon-offsetting services, green mortgages, green insurance, impact investing, microfinance, eco-friendly credit cards, and more.

Challenges for MSMEs in Accessing Green Finance

MSMEs are generally unaware of the need to prioritize decarbonization, green finance, and sustainability practices, which are key performance indicators for APEC economies. This lack of awareness keeps demand for them low, while information asymmetries keep supply low. Indeed, paradoxically, green finance could sometimes worsen the condition of MSMEs if barriers to their access are not addressed: these include lack of resources, costs, and reporting and compliance hurdles. APEC economies need to implement policies to overcome these barriers and to incentivize green finance products and services.

Policy Approaches to Support MSMEs' Access to Green Finance

APEC economies can develop four broad categories of policy approaches to support MSMEs and their access to green finance. First, they can introduce provision policies that ensure green-finance-type services are targeted and provided to MSMEs. Second, they can implement promotion policies to create incentives for the financial sector to deliver green-finance-related services. Third, they can provide protection policies to reduce financial risk by socializing potential losses through insurance or social-payment-based structures. Fourth, the private sector and government agencies can implement prevention policies and risk reduction measures that seek to avert undesirable outcomes for MSMEs before they happen.

In this report, Bank Indonesia's Carbon Calculator (Case Study 2) is highlighted as a practical policy initiative to help transition its economy away from carbon. The Carbon Calculator framework will support the green transformation for financial institutions, corporations, and MSMEs.

Green Finance for MSMEs to Address Food Security

Food systems represent about one-third of global carbon emissions and, therefore, green finance can play an important role in decarbonizing this critical industry sector. MSMEs are central in global food systems, which risk being unable to transition to a green economy. Green finance is thus critically important for MSMEs to decrease the likelihood of food insecurity (lack of availability), undernourishment, and food affordability.

Enabling MSME Green Finance Through Technology and Other Innovations

New technologies can ease MSME access to green finance solutions. Financial technology (fintech) can overcome the physical barriers and geographic impediments in some APEC economies (such as island economies) to deliver financial services, including to MSMEs. Such fintech services include mobile banking, e-wallets, person-to-person (P2P) lending, sustainable crowdfunding platforms, and others.[1] Other developments aiding green finance include decentralized electricity markets, carbon credits, and green bonds.

[1] See Box 2 in the main text.

Proposed Actions for Policymakers and Regulators

(i) Close knowledge gaps.

- Cooperate with the private sector and relevant institutions to support research into green financing and MSMEs, and to collect data from MSME-related pilot products and services.
- Work with stakeholders to expand green finance for MSMEs beyond the adoption of renewable energy or energy-efficient practices (e.g., carbon removal projects that have environmental and climate benefits).
- Develop economy-specific and regional road maps to transition to a cleaner economy, and identify priority areas for MSMEs and how green finance can support these road maps.
- Create regional and global depositories of knowledge for economies to share green finance and MSME experiences.
- Focus attention on green finance and MSME needs across industry sectors, with a specific focus on food security in the agriculture industry.

(ii) Improve inclusion of MSME issues in existing and new sustainable finance taxonomies and frameworks.

- Governments need to collaborate with industry associations and key stakeholders to examine how the various definitions of MSMEs align with current green taxonomies and what are the challenges for different MSME segments and industries.
- Include MSME-based projects and activities into green taxonomies, especially where they are users and suppliers of green technology and services.
- Incorporate climate adaptation and mitigation projects into green finance standards, including applicable transition financing.
- Consider the applicability and interoperability of taxonomies to meet MSME limitations (e.g., lack of collateral, lack of reporting ability) and specific sector needs (e.g., agriculture).

(iii) Steer financial service providers and MSMEs toward green finance opportunities through incentives and regulatory measures.

- Introduce and/or promote incentive schemes that specifically target the expansion of green finance in the MSME sector such as guidance to banks in green MSME lending.
- Develop more direct approaches for governments to interact with industry in green finance, such as encouraging state-owned banks to provide trade finance to MSMEs who meet green-related criteria. Governments can adopt preferential procurement from private sector MSMEs who employ green-related business practices.
- Develop incentive systems for financial institutions that support and encourage green MSME financing.
- Consider how existing government subsidy programs, for example, in the agriculture sector, can be tied to measurable indicators of green progress.

(iv) Embrace the development and application of fintech and new financial instruments.

- Develop regulations on compatibility and transferability of data (e.g., corporate environmental, social, and governance data) to facilitate greater cooperation between fintech service providers while providing clients the flexibility to switch or change service providers.
- Employ digital technology to enable MSMEs to automate data collection and verification processes and to meet green-finance-related disclosures (either voluntary and/or through mandatory reporting).
- Promote fintech and regulatory technology (regtech) to support the green finance functions of financial institutions that serve MSMEs.
- Grow and develop government funding schemes to support the fintech sector, such as startups, incubators, regulatory sandboxes, pilot programs, and more.
- Adopt regulations that enable innovative financial instruments to be developed that are relevant to MSMEs. Examples include but are not limited to microinsurance for climate disasters, biodiversity offsets, carbon credits, and more.
- Develop regulations to protect data privacy and security in relation to international data transfers and data sharing.

(v) Support capacity development among financial service providers, MSMEs, and other economic actors to adopt green finance.

- Work with relevant industry associations to identify needs and design appropriate interventions for MSMEs.
- Provide regular updates and training to MSMEs (through local government partners or digital means) on available green finance products and/or services and support mechanisms, as well as enhancing financial and digital literacy.
- Enable knowledge sharing among MSMEs and financial institutions through success cases and experiences of green MSME financing.
- Strengthen knowledge sharing on green technologies and green processes for MSMEs through roadshows, leaflets, digital means, etc. This information can include knowledge on green agriculture technologies, energy efficiency programs, the circular economy, etc.
- Foster cooperation and knowledge sharing among all stakeholders in the economy on the advantages and opportunities on green financing for MSMEs.

(vi) Develop comprehensive frameworks to leverage technology for expanding green finance access to MSMEs.

- Collaborate with the private sector to develop a green data framework based on open-banking principles, ensuring privacy and leveraging APEC guidelines for interoperable and secure systems.
- Enhance technology infrastructure, including cloud services and blockchain, and adopt open application programming interface (API) strategies with regulatory frameworks to expand green finance and ensure data protection.

- Encourage artificial intelligence adoption in green finance for tasks like credit scoring and environmental reporting through clear regulations and pilot programs that ensure transparency.
- Create innovation hubs and offer incentives, such as tax breaks and green bonds, to drive the development and adoption of green finance technologies.
- Build trust in green finance technologies through tailored digital education programs that integrate climate finance concepts for MSMEs.

1. Introduction

Micro, small, and medium-sized enterprises (MSMEs) significantly drive economic growth in developing economies, contributing to job creation and development of innovative products and services. Yet, the barriers are high to MSME access to financing opportunities, including their limited credit history and a lack of collateral (Cheok and Singh 2018). Businesses generally are facing surging financing needs as they navigate net-zero pathways and climate-resilient business models. This poses growing challenges to MSMEs in particular, which are largely constrained in their access to green finance.

Financial access and inclusion for MSMEs in green finance are therefore a critical issue for the Asia-Pacific Financial Inclusion Forum (APFIF) to address. The APFIF facilitates identification and development of concrete actions for policymakers and regulators to extend the reach and value of financial services to everyone, including those most in need.

The forum was established as a policy initiative on the recommendation of the Asia-Pacific Economic Cooperation (APEC) Business Advisory Council by the APEC Finance Ministers in 2010. Led by the Asian Development Bank (ADB), it aims to deliver the objectives of the Finance Ministers' Process related to financial inclusion.

To better understand challenges and opportunities for the green financing of MSMEs, ADB, in partnership with the Asian Development Bank Institute (ADBI) and with support from the Griffith Asia Institute, organized the 13th and 14th annual APFIF Policy Dialogues in Tokyo on 21–22 June 2023 and in Cusco on 30 May 2024. The meetings brought together senior government officials, policy experts, and industry leaders from multiple economies in Asia and the Pacific and Latin America.

Under the theme *"Policy Approaches to Support Green Financing of Micro, Small, and Medium-Sized Enterprises,"* the roundtable policy dialogues focused on identifying effective policy approaches to:

i. promote greater awareness and development of green finance products tailored to MSMEs,

ii. overcome the practical challenges MSMEs face in accessing green finance,

iii. address food insecurity by developing green finance opportunities for small-holder farmers, and

iv. expand green finance opportunities and effectiveness for MSMEs through innovative technology solutions.

Given the emergent nature of these issues and limited past work on them (Cheok and Singh 2018; OECD 2022; IGFWG 2022) the ADB teams designed a survey exploring the nexus between green finance and MSMEs. The survey was targeted at officials and roundtable participants from APEC economies between May and July 2023 and covered 16 questions in five broad themes.[2]

[2] The survey was distributed to officials of the 21 APEC economies, with responses collected between 5 May and 31 July 2023 from eight economies: the People's Republic of China, Indonesia, Japan, Malaysia, the Philippines, Mexico, Papua New Guinea, and Peru.

These themes explored respondents' perceptions of the (i) importance of green finance to MSMEs; (ii) barriers to accessing green finance in APEC economies; and (iii) policy approaches that might alleviate these barriers, and, more generally, improve access to green finance for MSMEs. Two further highly specific themes elicited respondents' perceptions of (iv) how access to green finance for MSMEs can help improve food security; and (v) how fintech and technology, in general, can alleviate barriers to MSMEs accessing green finance (described as "green fintech for MSMEs").

This publication reviews the nexus between green finance and MSMEs and recommends actions for policymakers and regulators identified through the policy dialogue and the survey. It also aims at connecting the perspective of MSME financing needs to the current discussions under the Finance Ministers' Process on sustainable finance, and the Sustainable Finance Initiative endorsed by APEC members in 2024. The proposed actions include steps to close the knowledge gap on how to expand the supply of green finance to MSMEs:

- defining the unique features of MSMEs within sustainable finance taxonomies and green finance frameworks;
- implementing incentives and regulatory measures to promote the enabling environment for green financing of MSMEs;
- facilitating the development of innovative technology solutions for green finance, including fintech; and
- supporting the capacity development of green finance stakeholders from both supply- and demand-side perspectives.

These proposed actions align with broader efforts in Asia and the Pacific for supporting the MSME green transition (ADB 2025) and efforts within the Finance Ministers' Process to accelerate financial inclusion as a priority area of the Incheon Plan endorsed by APEC members in 2025, as well as to advance APEC's Putrajaya Vision 2040, which calls for greater progress in achieving inclusion and sustainability for the region.

2. What Is Green Finance?

Interest in sustainable, green, environmental, and climate finance has risen in recent years. But before discussing the importance of green finance to MSMEs, these key terms need to be defined. ADB (2024) provides a useful scheme for doing so (Figure 1). Sustainable finance is the broadest term and is concerned with environmental, social, and governance (ESG) issues, primarily throughout the risk management and investment decision-making process (Bakken 2021; UNEP 2016). "Environmental" factors may relate to finance and investment, and are commonly associated with *green finance* (ADB 2021). Related issues include concerns with climate change and use of sustainable resources. "Social factors" are associated with *impact finance* (ADB 2021). Examples include concerns about human and/or animal and protecting consumer interests. "Governance" is concerned with how public and private organizations are governed (for example, employee relations, compensation practices, corporate social responsibility, board/executive governance, and more) and is associated with *stakeholder finance* (ADB 2021). Finally, Figure 1 highlights, through the inclusion of the term "economic," that ESG cannot come at the expense of economic development; rather it should enhance economic outcomes.

In broad terms, green finance can be defined as a subset of sustainable finance (Figure 1). However, because of the general nature of this concept, a standard or unifying definition of green finance is not straightforward. Some stakeholders specify the various types of financial segments, instruments, and institutions in their definition of green finance, while others tend to keep it broad. For example, the World Economic Forum (Fleming 2020) defines green finance as "any structured financial activity that has been created to ensure a better environmental outcome." The Alliance for Financial Inclusion (AFI 2022) uses a concept that includes environmental degradation and a more precise approach to mitigation and adaptation. The OECD (2023) defines the related concept of green growth as activities to achieve "economic growth while reducing pollution and greenhouse gas emissions, minimizing waste, and improving efficiency in the use of natural resources." "Environment finance," meanwhile, is broadly equivalent to green finance.

Green finance, in turn, has climate finance as one of its subsets. Climate finance, broadly defined, is concerned with adaptation finance and mitigation finance. Adaptation finance is concerned with developing resilient infrastructure and assets to deal with rising physical risks that may be increasing in frequency and severity due to climate change (e.g., flooding, wildfires, etc.), while mitigation and transition finance are concerned with achieving low-carbon economies in line with international agreements such as the Paris Agreement. These concepts are related to the Taskforce on Climate-related Financial Disclosures (TCFD 2022) risk framework adopted by economies and financial institutions seeking to understand climate change-related risks to financial systems, investors, and firms through the lens of physical, transition, and liability risks.

Figure 1: Defining Sustainable, Green, and Climate Finance

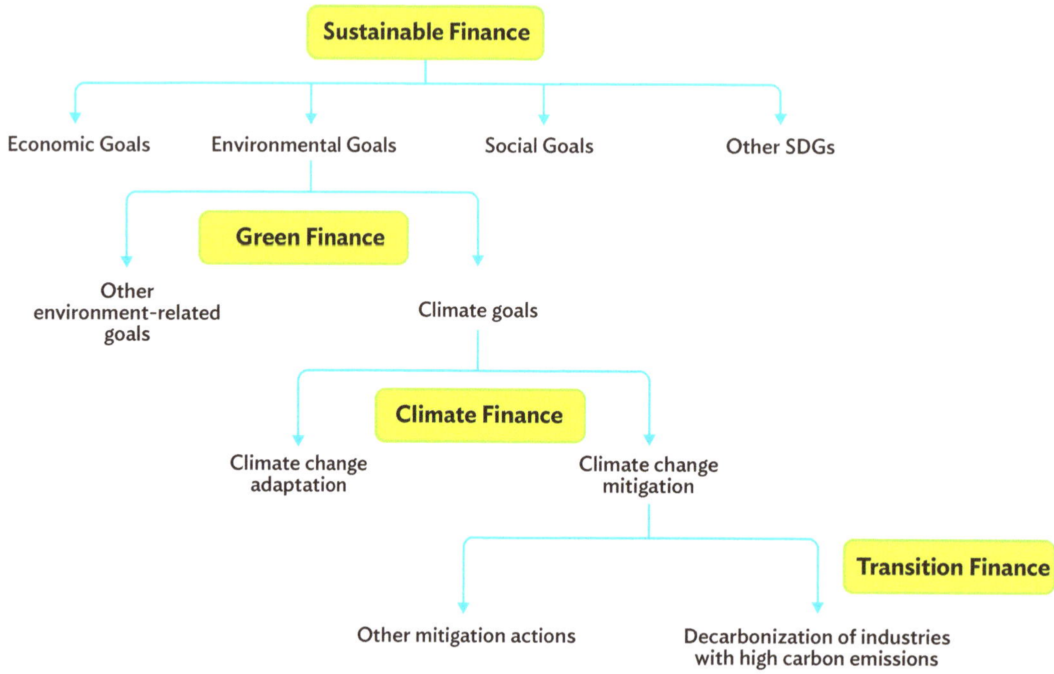

SDG = Sustainable Development Goal.
Source: ADB. 2024. *Asia-Pacific Climate Report 2024: Catalyzing Finance and Policy Solutions.*

Several rationales and motivations incentivize green finance in an economy. First, green finance can assist economies as they reduce carbon intensiveness. A less carbon-intensive economy means that economic growth can increase (i.e., gross domestic product [GDP]) with minimal or lower overall negative effects on the environment). Second, economies with UN Sustainable Development Goals (SDGs) commitments can achieve these objectives more quickly if green finance is deployed to transform the structure of their economies.

From the perspective of thematic investment typologies, UNEP (2016) developed a grouping methodology to classify types of green finance and investment (Figure 2). The groupings reveal that green finance and investment encapsulate many aspects of a broader economy. The figure also highlights the many "shades" of green, by the "most commonly included" as dark green and the "least commonly included" as light green or white. This relates to how unambiguously each technology or practice is seen as green, with, for instance, wind and solar power nearly always regarded as green, while "clean"' coal with carbon capture and storage is infrequently regarded as green due to technological and economic challenges associated with that latter technology. This concern with what qualifies as green, in turn, can be used in green finance products and services (Box 1) and has led to the development of green taxonomies and green banking frameworks internationally, which include the European Union Green Taxonomy (European Commission 2023), the Association of Southeast Asian Nations (ASEAN) Taxonomy for Sustainable Finance (ASEAN 2023), and the People's Republic of China green banking framework (Case Study 3). A key challenge for Asia and the Pacific is going to be the harmonization of these frameworks and taxonomies to keep compliance costs low and thereby unlock trillions of dollars for green transition and climate resilience (Um 2023).

Figure 2: Many Shades of Green Finance

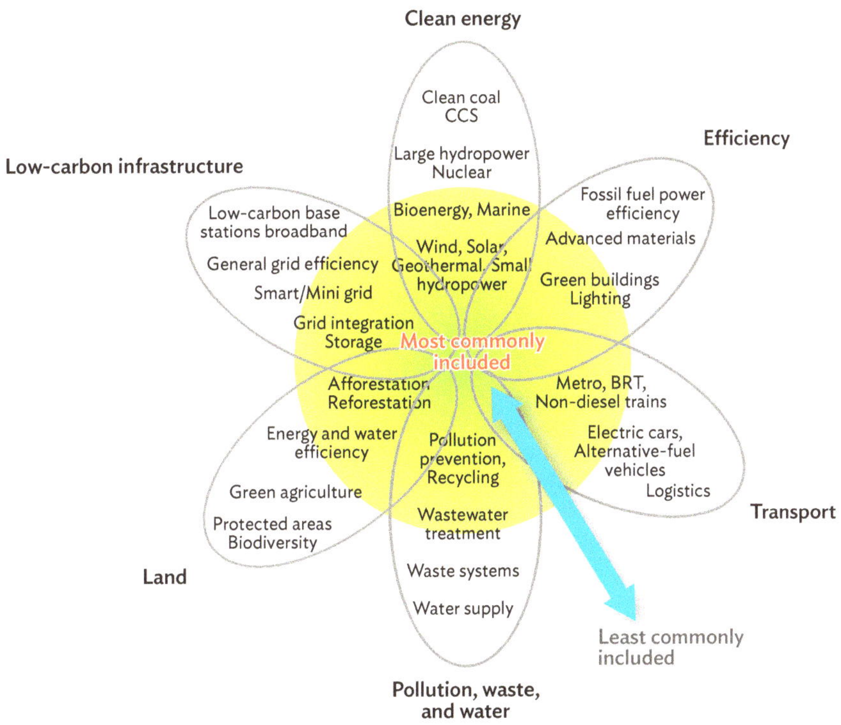

BRT = bus rapid transit, CCS = carbon capture and storage.
Source: UNEP 2016.

Box 1 presents examples of green finance products and services supporting MSMEs to have a positive impact on the environment. Governments need to incentivize their development.

Box 1: Green Finance Products and Services

Green bonds: These are debt securities issued by governments, municipalities, or corporations to fund environment-friendly projects such as renewable energy projects, energy efficiency improvements, sustainable infrastructure, and clean transportation.[a]

Renewable energy financing: Financial products and services that provide funding for the development, installation, and operation of renewable energy projects, including solar, wind, hydroelectric, and geothermal energy.[b]

Energy efficiency loans: Loans specifically designed to help individuals, businesses, and institutions invest in energy-efficient technologies and improvements, such as energy-efficient appliances, building retrofits, and efficient lighting systems.[c]

Sustainable funds: Investment funds that focus on companies or projects with strong environmental, social, and governance practices. These funds may avoid investing in industries with negative impacts on the environment or society.

continued on the next page

Box 1 continued

Carbon-offsetting services: Financial products that allow individuals and companies to offset their carbon emissions by investing in projects that reduce or capture an equivalent amount of carbon dioxide from the atmosphere, such as reforestation or carbon capture projects.[d]

Green mortgages: Mortgage products that offer lower interest rates or other incentives to individuals who purchase energy-efficient homes or make eco-friendly improvements to their existing properties.[e]

Green insurance: Insurance products that provide coverage for environmentally focused risks, such as disasters caused by climate change, or that incentivize environmentally responsible behaviors through premium discounts.[f]

Impact investing: Investment strategies that prioritize both financial returns and positive social or environmental impacts. This can include investments in sectors like affordable housing, clean water, education, and health care.[g]

Microfinance for sustainable development: Microfinance institutions that offer financial services to low-income individuals and communities for sustainable development projects, such as clean water access, renewable energy, and agriculture.[h]

Eco-friendly credit cards: Credit cards that donate a portion of the spending to environmental causes, offer rewards for sustainable purchases, or offset the cardholder's carbon footprint.[i]

Green leases: Leasing arrangements that encourage energy efficiency and sustainable practices in commercial buildings, often through shared cost savings between tenants and landlords.[j]

Sustainable investment advisory services: Financial advisory services that help individuals and institutions align their investment portfolios with their values and sustainability goals.

[a] Dembele, Schwarz and Horrocks (2021); Greitens (2023).
[b] Elie, Granier, and Rigot (2021); Painuly and Wohlgemuth (2006).
[c] Katris and Turner (2021).
[d] Hendrichs and Busch (2012).
[e] Gifford (2018); ICG Consulting Canada Inc. (2007).
[f] Lee and Fung (2023); Hu et al. (2023); Nie and Li (2017).
[g] Lamptey and Ngoasong (2023).
[h] Brown, Guin, and Kirschemann (2016); Dorfleitner, Nguyen, and Rohe (2019).
[i] Bihari and Pandey (2015).
[j] Collins and Junghans (2015).
Source: Authors.

3. Importance of Green Finance to MSMEs in APEC Economies

Since its inception in 1993, APEC (2023a) has championed sustainability as vital for long-term economic advancement, with the APEC Economic Leaders' Statement noting that "our environment is improved as we protect the quality of our air, water, and green spaces and manage our energy resources and renewable resources to ensure sustainable growth and provide a more secure future for our people." The organization's commitment to addressing climate and the environment has continued through initiatives such as the APEC Climate Center and the Sydney Declaration (APEC 2007). APEC's ambitious goal to reduce energy intensity by 45% before 2035 is projected to be achieved by 2029 (APEC 2023b). Further, the need for "strong, sustainable, inclusive, and balanced growth" has been reasserted via the Finance Ministers' Process and the Cebu Action Plan (APEC 2023c), which also note the need for enhanced financial resilience to mitigate the risks of disasters caused by natural hazards. In recent years, APEC has focused green finance discussions on areas such as urban energy transition (APEC 2023d) and infrastructure development (APEC 2018).

For instance, APEC (2023d) emphasized that ESG and especially green taxonomies can help bridge the "climate finance gap" (the difference between current investment rates and what is needed to mitigate the worst effects of climate change). Further, the report noted that, for increasing the resilience of cities, credit risk guarantees, environmental insurance, and catastrophe or CAT bonds are the critical instruments. On the nexus between sustainability and MSMEs, Cheok and Singh (2018) identify barriers to greater sustainability of MSMEs, including the following:

- Lack of awareness of the environmental impact of their activities.
- Limited use of information and communication technology in becoming more sustainable.
- Challenges in understanding and adapting to changing regulatory environments.
- Green skills and competency gaps.
- Challenges in accessing finance, especially when investing in innovative technological solutions.
- Barriers to accessing green markets, due to their complex and rapidly changing nature.

This report, including the policy dialogue and ADB survey underpinning it, complements this existing APEC knowledge base by focusing on MSMEs in the green finance context. It presents APEC's sustainability and financial inclusion efforts in the context of MSMEs. To understand how green finance and MSMEs intersect, the study proposes a conceptual model of the green finance and MSME nexus (Figure 3). Green finance can be a paradox for MSMEs and economies where they concentrate, as Figure 3 and the following discussion make clear.

Figure 3: Green Finance and MSME Nexus

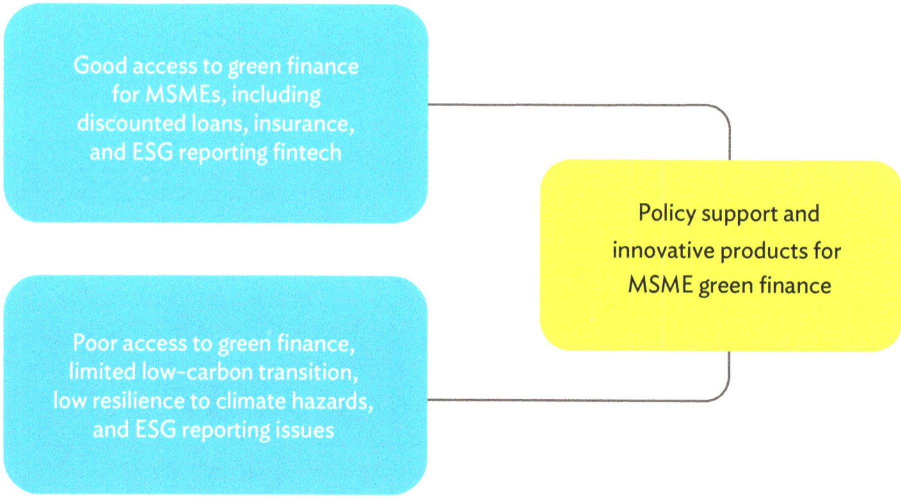

ESG = environmental, social, and governance; fintech = financial technology; MSME = micro, small, and medium-sized enterprise.
Source: Authors.

On the one hand, inadequate access to green finance due to unfavorable treatment of MSMEs could deteriorate economic and sustainable development indicators. Without access to green loans (e.g., microfinance) and insurance products, MSMEs will struggle to transition to a low-carbon economy, and their businesses will not be resilient to climate shocks. The Table identifies and elaborates on four main barriers, and potential solutions, to MSMEs accessing green finance:

- transition design;
- ESG measurement, reporting, and verification challenges;
- product availability; and
- information problems.

The first and the last two are highly intuitive, but ESG measurement, reporting, and verification challenges merit further explanation. They relate to how challenges in reporting ESG metrics may mean MSMEs get locked out of supply chains by larger international companies that once bought their products. For instance, due to investor pressure or as a result of regulations, an increasing number of multinational enterprises must report their carbon footprints, including direct emissions (scope 1 emissions), emissions from purchased electricity (scope 2 emissions), and up- and down-stream supply chain emissions (scope 3 emissions) (Nguyen, Diaz-Rainey, and Kuruppuarachchi 2021; Nguyen et al. 2023). Thus, many multinational enterprises are asking their supply chains to report emissions, which is costly for most businesses, particularly MSMEs, which may lack expertise or financial resources to report this metric. And MSMEs may be asked to report even more metrics as sustainability regulatory requirements increase globally (see taxonomies in section 2). This may leave big enterprises reluctant to engage MSMEs.

Table: MSME Access to Green Finance—Barriers and Solutions

Barriers	Potential Solutions
Transition design: MSMEs are not considered in green finance market development. This can result in policies and products not catering to MSME needs, e.g., insufficient capital, labor shortages, unskilled workers. This leads to lack of supply of appropriate green finance products for MSMEs.	**Inclusive green finance road maps:** When developing green finance road maps, MSME representation and considerations are critical, so that these road maps develop policy and products that account for their particular needs. For instance, MSMEs may need microfinance to be explicitly considered in green finance road maps.
ESG measurement, reporting, and verification challenges: No support for MSMEs in this area. This can leave MSMEs unable to report critical ESG factors and cut out of supply chains or markets. This is relevant to a range of ESG metrics but multinational enterprises seeking to report scope 3 emissions may be the most relevant example (see main text). This may reduce demand for MSME products that cannot report their emissions and lead to lower margins for these products.	**Technology to the rescue:** Financial and regulatory technologies can be used to make measurement, reporting, and verification of ESG metrics low-cost and easily understood. Case Study 2 provides an example of such a tool, in which Bank Indonesia has created a carbon calculator to support the measurement of scopes 1, 2, and 3 emissions in financial institutions, corporations, and MSMEs.
Product availability: Low profitability or high risk of MSMEs green finance products: Even if MSMEs can report ESG metrics with the help of financial technology (fintech) andregulatory technology (regtech), financial institutions may be unwilling to provide green finance products (see Box 1) as they may see them as riskier and/or less profitable in the context of MSMEs. This will lead to a lack of supply of green finance products for MSMEs.	**Policy support to incentivize green finance products and transition for MSMEs:** Policymakers can use a range of provision, promotion, prevention, and protection policies to ensure MSMEs have adequate access to green finance products (see section 5). This can include tax or financial incentives that MSMEs, or MSME financial service providers, receive to incentivize MSMEs to "green" their production. This can include loans, trade finance, and insurance guarantees contingent on specific 'greening' measures.
Information problems: MSMEs not consulted or informed of green finance products. Even if there are appropriate green finance products for MSMEs, they may be unaware of them or have a poor understanding of the benefits, and thus leave demand lacking.	**Information and education:** Policymakers can implement or help nongovernment organizations implement a range of information, education, and capacity-building interventions to enhance MSME awareness of green finance products and their benefits, the latter potentially including attracting a broader customer base and higher margins via higher environmental standards.

ESG = environmental, social, and governance; MSME = micro, small, and medium-sized enterprise.
Source: Authors.

As outlined in the Table, inclusive road maps, government policies to incentivize access to innovative and comprehensive green finance products, information campaigns, and enabling information and communication technology (e.g., green fintech and regtech used to measure, manage, and report ESG metrics) can help overcome barriers to MSME access of green finance. For example, Thailand has implemented complementary initiatives to drive both digitalization and green transition among MSMEs (Case Study 1). Such approaches will lead to more resilient and environmentally and financially sustainable MSMEs, with associated improvements in income standards and higher SDG attainment in economies highly dependent on MSMEs.

Figure 4: Importance of Green Finance to MSMEs
(%)

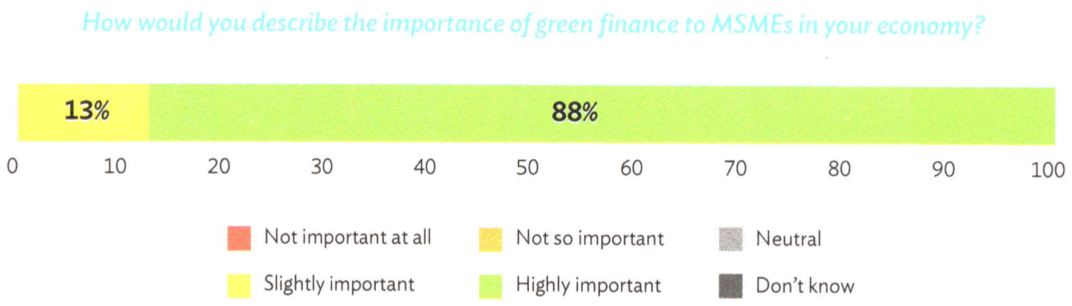

MSMEs = micro, small, and medium-sized enterprises.
Source: ADB Nexus between Green Finance and MSMEs survey result.

The importance of green finance to MSMEs is high for almost all APEC economies that responded to the survey (Figure 4). And respondent APEC economies believe this nexus is particularly relevant to certain sectors: general manufacturing, agriculture, textiles, retail, and heavy industry (Figure 5). Many of these are likely to be export-oriented industries, suggesting that green finance challenges may come from external pressures (e.g., supply chain ESG reporting pressures).

This report, in section 6, focuses on food security as an important theme in the green finance and MSME nexus. Agriculture is likely to have many microenterprises that are critical to food security within less developed APEC economies.

Figure 5: Relevance of Green Finance to MSME Industries

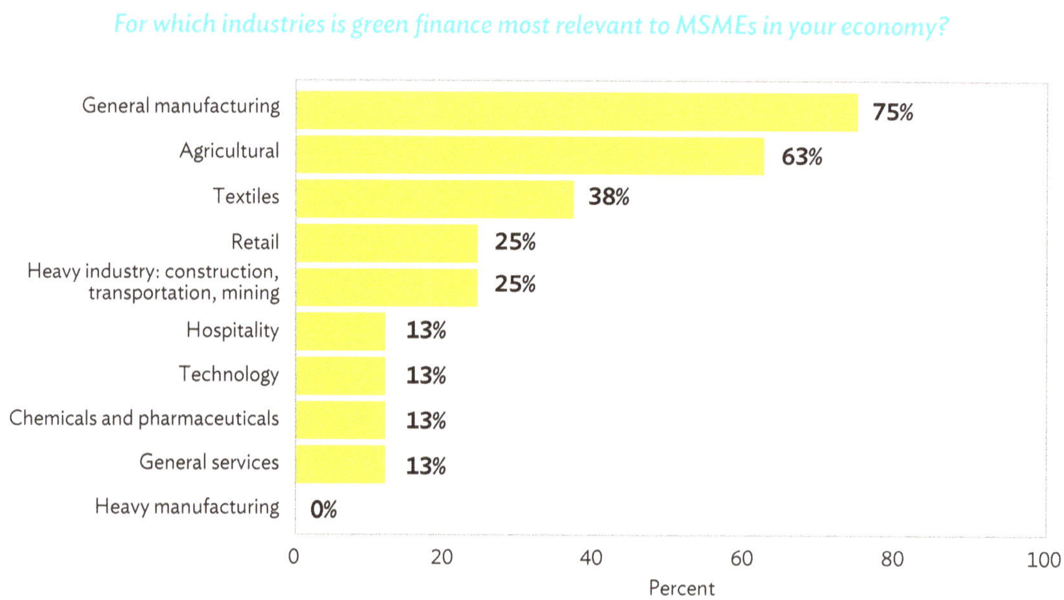

MSME = micro, small, and medium-sized enterprise.
Source: ADB Nexus between Green Finance and MSMEs survey result.

Box 2: Case Study 1—Thailand's Policies for a Digitized and Green Economy

About 8–9 years ago, Thailand's Ministry of Industry launched a green transformation campaign. A majority of large and medium-sized firms linking to global supply chains are already on board with the green transformation initiative.

Small and medium-sized enterprises (SMEs) have experienced numerous crises over the past 15 years, including the 2008 Global Financial Crisis, the 2011 "Great Flood" in across a vast swathe of land north of Bangkok, political polarization and conflict (among so-called red and yellow shirt supporters), the coronavirus disease (COVID-19) pandemic, and high energy prices at present.

Yet, SMEs need to prioritize growing their businesses. At the moment, the high priority for SMEs is "digital transformation," which was brought to the fore during the COVID-19 pandemic. If SMEs do not complete transformation to the digital economy, individuals and businesses are likely to be cut off from many markets. Current statistics show that 34.6% of Thailand's gross domestic product is generated from SMEs and 3.2 million SMEs employ 71% of Thai workers.

To foster and nurture a green transformation, therefore, Thailand has implemented initiatives to enable SMEs to access green finance. The country aims at an environment-friendly economy through the so-called Bio-Circular-Green model. The Government of Thailand expects to transform to a green and digitized economy by implementing the following initiatives:

i. In 2023, the Government of Thailand introduced the "'SME Master Plan 2023–2027" with a focus on a post-COVID-19 strategy on a Bio-Circular-Green model to adopt a green transformation pathway. This master plan sends a strong signal to both public and private sectors of the government's intention toward a green transformation.
ii. The government currently enforces the "SME Integrated Budget System." All government agencies (i.e., 10 ministries and 100 agencies) responsible for SME promotion are expected to develop a budget allocation for digital transformation together with green transformation. If government agencies do not allocate budget funding to digital transformation or Bio-Circular-Green transformation, then it is most likely that the government agency seeking funding will not receive an approved budget.
iii. The Bank of Thailand has also worked closely with the Thailand Bankers' Association and Securities and Exchange Commission to circulate green financing into the economy and have large companies assist SMEs in their supply chains so they can progress along their green transformation journey.

Overall, the digital transformation of the economy of Thailand is a first priority, followed by the green transformation of private and publics sectors. The implementation of the Thai government's SME Promotion Master Plan 2023–2027 and SME Integrated Budget System will significantly contribute to the realization of a digitized and green economy.

Source: Authors.

4. Challenges for MSMEs in Accessing Green Finance

As explained in section 2, green finance is offered only to corporate activities that improve green outcomes, increasingly as defined by green taxonomies and green banking frameworks (Case Study 3). Without MSMEs becoming more aware of sustainability issues such as decarbonization, green finance cannot be a viable financing option for MSMEs (Cheok and Singh 2018). Fifty percent of APEC economies responding to the survey noted that demand for green finance is low among MSMEs due to low awareness of this financing option.

Figure 6: Additional Reporting Requirements of Green Finance

Question 1: How difficult is it for MSMEs in your economy to meet the additional reporting requirements and reporting costs associated with green finance (i.e., ESG metrics such as carbon footprint reporting)?

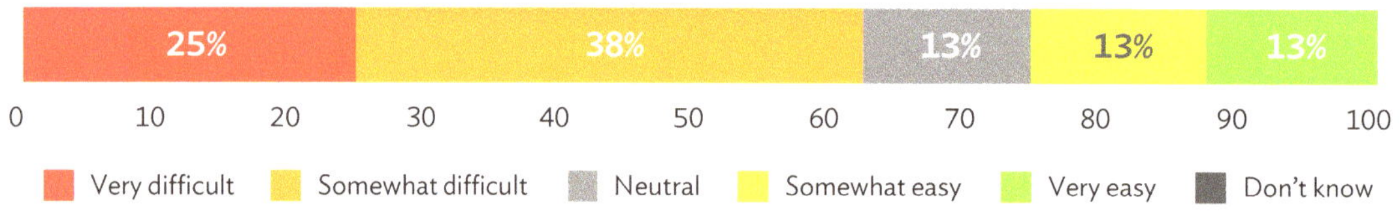

Question 2: Large companies are increasingly reluctant to engage with MSMEs in your economy because MSMEs are unable to report ESG metrics and fulfill ESG requirements. For example, tracking carbon footprint (E), board diversity (G), and fair-trade policy (S).

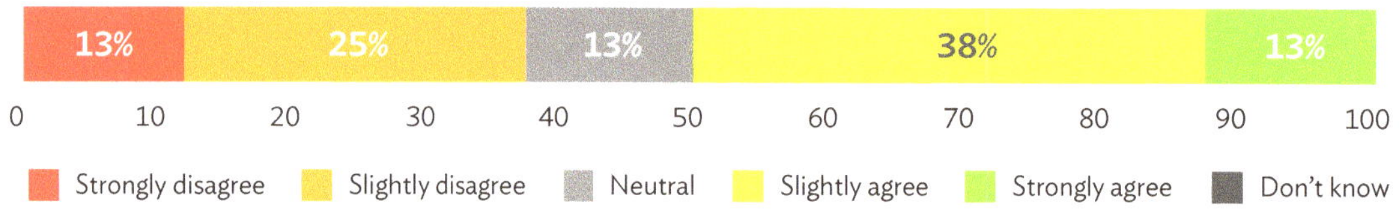

ESG = environmental, social, and governance; MSME = micro, small, and medium-sized enterprise.
Source: ADB Nexus between Green Finance and MSMEs survey result.

Figure 7: Status of Green Finance Products Among MSMEs

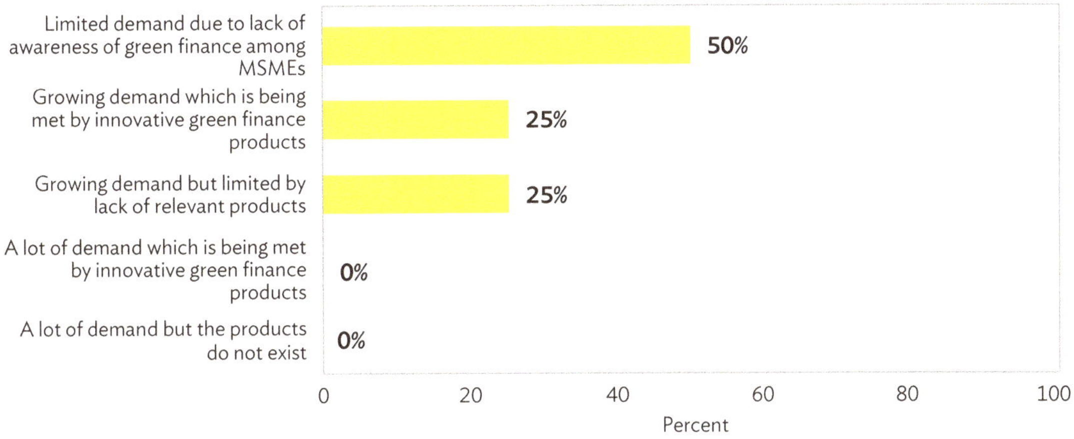

MSMEs = micro, small, and medium-sized enterprises.
Source: ADB Nexus between Green Finance and MSMEs survey result.

Limitations on Available Resources and Their Cost

Green finance rules require capital raisers to report the green activities they are financing. Current sustainable reporting frameworks (including the Taskforce on Climate-related Financial Disclosures, Green Taxonomies, green banking frameworks, ESG metrics) use a complex matrix comprising nonfinancial factors, which requires employees with sufficient capacity and capability to handle them. The matrix is not designed for small entities, and, for this reason, the data may not be readily collectable by them. Unlike large entities, MSMEs have limited resources (i.e., human, monetary, and data) to measure and report the environmental impact of their activities.

Further, many of the challenges explained above also apply to the supply side of green finance (i.e., financial institutions and microfinance institutions). Under green finance rules, a certain activity or information needs to be reported by a company only if it has a material impact on the environment. However, material activities greatly vary from company to company, and financial institutions may not have the relevant resources or capacity to guide and monitor MSMEs on this. Financial institutions may not have sufficient capability to analyze data supplied by client MSMEs. This might be particularly true for small microfinance institutions serving small enterprises. Even if they do, the green finance market for MSMEs may not be large enough to allocate adequate resources. This incentive issue also makes financial institutions less inclined to expand their green finance product line for MSMEs.

All the above suggest greater transaction costs of green finance for MSMEs, be it from the demand side (borrowers) or the supply side (lenders). To emphasize this, 63% of APEC member respondents felt that MSMEs in their economies found it difficult or very difficult to meet the additional reporting requirements and reporting costs associated with green finance (see Figure 6, question 1). Further, 38% of responding APEC economies believe MSMEs inability to report ESG metrics may be making large companies reluctant to engage with them (see Figure 6, question 2). Related to this, a survey conducted by ADB on trade finance gaps shows that both banks and companies believe that ESG alignment will reduce the time and cost of credit approval process of SMEs (ADB 2023). If this is the case, then inability to report ESG metrics could have real economic impact. This is consistent with the green finance–MSME nexus paradox (see Figure 3).

Figure 8: Barriers to MSME Access to Green Finance Instruments

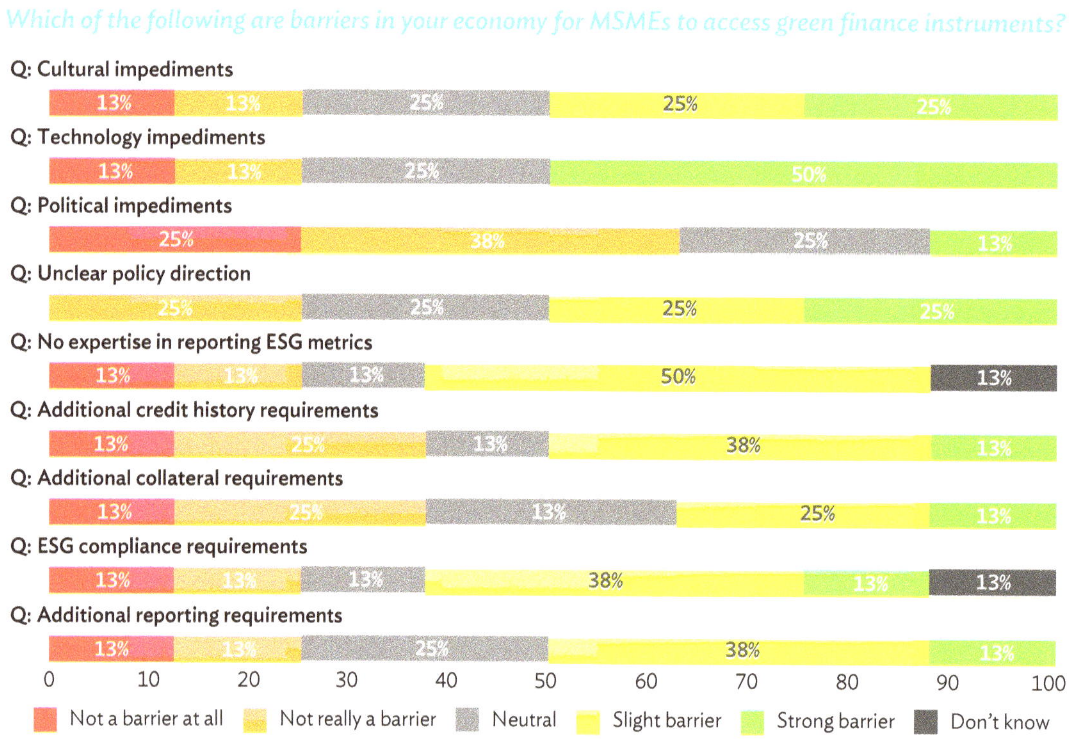

ESG = environmental, social, and governance; MSME = micro, small, and medium-sized enterprise.
Source: ADB Nexus between Green Finance and MSMEs survey result.

These challenges were discussed during the 2023 APFIF Policy Dialogue and some efforts to overcome them were shared by officials from the member economies. For example, Bank Indonesia, in collaboration with relevant ministries and institutions, has developed a carbon calculator tool to support financial institutions and corporations including MSMEs on the measurement of scopes 1, 2, and 3 emissions (Case Study 2). Further, proposed actions 1, 2, and 5, formulated from the dialogue discussions and documented later in this report, can help member economies address these challenges.

Barriers Recognized by APEC Economies

To better understand the paradox, the ADB Nexus between Green Finance and MSMEs survey explored potential barriers to green finance for MSMEs. Potential barriers are presented in Figure 7, and it is evident that there are many. "No experience in reporting ESG metrics," "ESG compliance requirements," and "additional reporting requirement" are all perceived as important barriers, perhaps not surprisingly given the results from the survey (see Figure 6). Notably, cultural and, in particular, technological impediments, are also seen as a significant negative impact on MSMEs accessing green finance and related instruments. This possibility is explored in section 7.

A second category of barriers is more financial in nature. For instance, around half of respondent APEC economies felt that "additional credit history requirement" may be an impediment —though it is not entirely clear if this is true just of green finance issues or a more general finance issue for MSMEs (Cheok and

Singh 2018). Further, approximately 40% of respondents identify collateral as a barrier. The absence of suitable collateral prevents MSMEs from accessing formal funding sources (Figure 8). According to previous research, 78% of the capital stock of MSMEs consists of movable assets like apparatus and equipment (Burns 2022). However, financial institutions require immovable assets, such as land or structures, as collateral. Consequently, MSMEs frequently rely on collateral-free informal sources of financing, such as family and acquaintances. This is limiting, as access to financing will depend on a person's network rather than the quality of their endeavor. Others rely on informal moneylenders, who frequently employ usurious interest rates and unregulated, aggressive debt collection methods.

The final set of barriers relate to politics and policy. That "political impediments" is not seen as a barrier in general suggests that governments generally provide adequate support for green finance and that the barriers are, as discussed, more cost, informational, and financial in nature. This is not to say that policy as distinct from politics is not a barrier, with around half of respondents suggesting that "unclear policy direction" could be an issue.

Box 3: Case Study 2—Indonesia's Carbon Calculator

Bank Indonesia recognizes climate-related risks and how they can evolve into multidimensional risks and challenges. Climate risk manifesting in extreme weather events increases the probability of physical risks (e.g., storms, floods, wildfires, rising sea levels, etc.). These negative externalities (or effects) will have a stronger impact on the poorest and marginalized individuals. Bank Indonesia is developing policy actions in the financial sector and with micro, small, and medium-sized enterprises (MSMEs) as a priority as they are the most vulnerable sector exposed to the adverse impacts of transition risk. These new policy actions are designed to ensure a balanced and healthy banking intermediation environment under the Indonesian macroprudential policy framework.

To manage the transition to a less carbon-intensive economy, Bank Indonesia has outlined three key strategies for promoting net-zero emissions: (i) to support firms in measuring their carbon emissions to be disclosed in their sustainability reports, (ii) to encourage banks in measuring carbon emissions of their loan portfolios, and (iii) to incentivize banks in aligning their green financing portfolio with the transition agenda. These strategies take into account both banking and firm perspectives (supply-demand sides) by promoting the role of banks in green finance and green transformation among borrowers. These strategies provide a foundation for shaping "green macroprudential policy," including the development of a supporting tool referred to as the Carbon Calculator.

The Carbon Calculator is a measurement tool developed by Bank Indonesia in collaboration with other ministries/institutions, designed to facilitate green finance and to encourage lower carbon emissions. The Carbon Calculator will gradually facilitate the measurement of scopes 1, 2, and 3 emissions in financial institutions, corporations, and MSMEs. More specifically, the Carbon Calculator tool will require banks to estimate their debtors' carbon emissions proportionally. The Carbon Calculator aims to motivate banks to lower the carbon emissions of their portfolio by increasing their lending activities to green finance activities. The Carbon Calculator initiative will be voluntary and incur zero cost to participants. This initiative will support building a comparable and open-access data repository, strengthen authorities' ability to assess climate-related risks and their implications for financial stability, and provide valuable inputs for policy development.

Overall, the Carbon Calculator will support Indonesia in transitioning to a lower carbon-intensive economy over the short to medium term. It is expected that the sources of emission reduction and avoidance will stem from projects including solar panel generation, wind power, water turbine generation, electric vehicles, carbon reduction certificates, green bonds, and others. Indonesia's transition to a green economy (supported by the Carbon Calculator) will reduce the negative externalities on MSMEs and incentivize financial institutions to offer green finance solutions to both MSMEs and larger-sized businesses.

Source: Authors.

5. Policy Approaches to Support MSME Access to Green Finance

Section 2 highlighted the several important disclosure and policy-related initiatives emerging internationally in the green finance space, including the Taskforce on Climate-related Financial Disclosures, green taxonomies, and green banking frameworks (Case Study 3). Further, a growing number of innovative green finance products and services are available that can help transform economies (see section 2 and Box 1). However, as noted in section 4, MSMEs face multiple barriers to accessing green finance. Green finance also has the potential to harm MSMEs though additional reporting costs or losing access to markets if they fail to report ESG metrics.

The rapid expansion of green finance products through better customization for the MSME sector, as well as the development of processes required to improve access to green finance, has the potential to unlock both finance and green development opportunities for businesses operating in this underserved market. Policymakers and regulators play a crucial role in attaining this objective by fostering an environment conducive to green financing for MSMEs (see Figure 3).

The Alliance for Financial Inclusion (2020) categorizes policies and regulations to address MSME sustainability and green financing into four groups:

- **Provision policies:** These aid governments in ensuring financial services are provided to eligible recipients, either directly or by the private sector carrying out a government mandate. Provision policies that address climate change and MSMEs can target adaptation and mitigation activities for MSMEs and involve mandating lending or targeted distribution of funds provided directly or indirectly to MSMEs through financial institutions.
- **Promotion policies:** Government promotion policies entail incentives for the private sector to provide financial services to eligible beneficiaries. Incentives for MSMEs may be nonfinancial and frequently include capacity building, knowledge sharing, and data collection. The accumulation of data has become an important topic for regulators seeking to better comprehend and communicate climate risks to the financial sector.
- **Protection policies:** These reduce financial risk by "socializing" potential losses through insurance or social payments or by granting exceptional access to an individual's assets. Protection policies focus primarily on adaptive measures for MSMEs in response to an unexpected extreme climatic event or in anticipation of adverse changes in weather conditions. Consequently, protection policies enable MSMEs to adapt to these risks.
- **Prevention policies:** These aim to avert undesirable outcomes, as opposed to addressing them after the fact. For MSMEs, prevention policies address the internalization and management of long- and short-term socio-environmental risks to or by MSMEs through the promotion of risk reduction measures by policymakers, regulators, and the private sector. This is most observed in guidelines for environmental and social risk management.

Within this context, and to better understand which green finance products and policies were implemented in APEC economies in general and specifically for MSMEs, the ADB Nexus between Green Finance and MSMEs survey included several related questions. From Figure 9, results indicate that, for economies responding to the survey, green loans were the most prevalent green finance product (88%), followed by green insurance (38%). In policies, Figure 10 summarizes which instruments receive policy support and which policy measures have been implemented both generally and specifically for MSMEs. In general interventions, policy support for green and sustainable bonds, green loans, and renewable energy investment were most common.

The results for this limited set of respondents suggest far fewer policy interventions are targeted at MSMEs. Further, those interventions targeted or adapted for MSMEs are quite different to conventional policies. For instance, green taxonomies were implemented in 20% of responding economies, but in no cases were these taxonomies adapted for the MSME context, which may inadvertently impede MSMEs access to green finance. Encouragingly, policy support for green insurance and microfinance was more common for MSMEs than green finance in general, although absolute levels of support seemed low (e.g., only 10% of respondent economies provided support for green insurance for MSMEs). There is clearly a scope for more policy support targeted at MSME green finance products and services. While the survey results provide guidance on the provision of green finance for MSMEs, they call for more research to understand the needs and level of policy support required.

Figure 9: Green Finance Instruments in APEC Respondent Economies

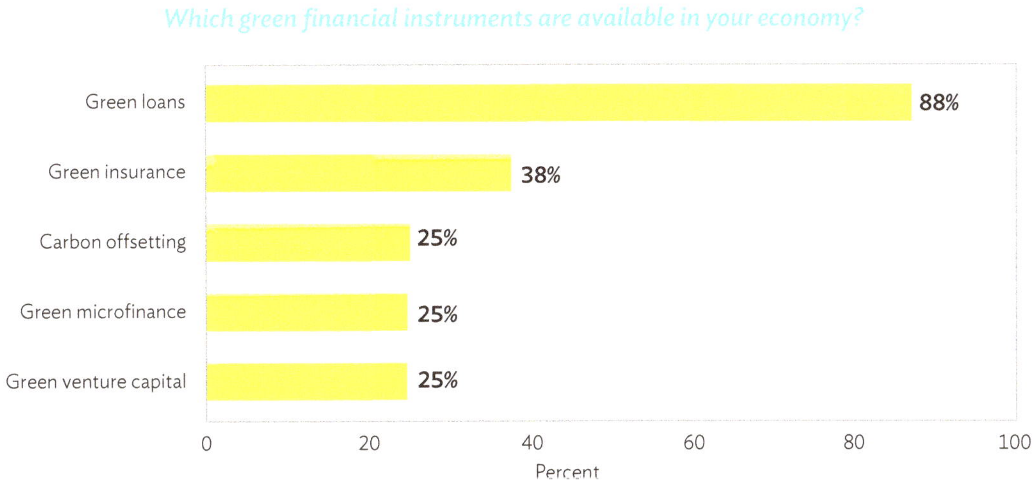

APEC = Asia-Pacific Economic Cooperation.
Source: ADB Nexus between Green Finance and MSMEs survey result.

Figure 10: Policy Support for Green Instruments for All Firms and MSMEs

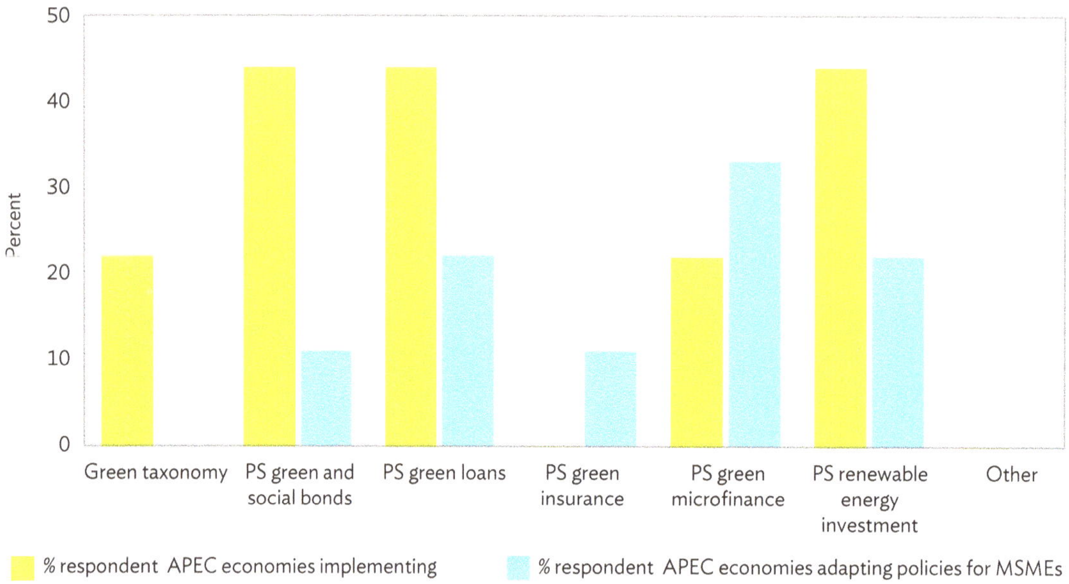

APEC = Asia-Pacific Economic Cooperation; MSME = micro, small, and medium-sized enterprise; PS = policy support.
Source: ADB Nexus between Green Finance and MSMEs survey result.

Box 4: Case Study 3—The People's Republic of China and Its Innovative Guidelines

Since 2007, the People's Republic of China (PRC) has developed three green-finance-related guidelines as a strategy to reshape its economy. These guidelines are as follows:

i. Credit Underwriting for Energy Conservation and Emission Reduction

In 2007, the PRC published its first set of guidelines related to credit underwriting for energy conservation and emission reduction. These guidelines were initiated for financial institutions to develop financial support for corporations to help them save energy and reduce emissions. These guidelines also define the responsibilities of the boards and senior management of financial institutions to assist corporates in their efforts to save energy and reduce emissions. This initiative also encourages financial institutions to reduce and prevent environmental risks associated with energy-intensive industries. The 2007 guidelines assist financial institutions to provide financial support to energy-efficient projects launched by energy users—client companies themselves or subcontracted by them to third-party energy service companies. Under these arrangements, an energy service company can pledge the cash flows earned from energy saving to banking-based financial institutions as a form of collateral. This initiative means there is a higher probability that micro, small, and medium-sized enterprises (MSMEs) will utilize green energy in the future.

ii. Green Credit Guidelines

In 2012, the PRC published its second set of guidelines, known as the Green Credit Guidelines, based on the following three pillars:

a. support green, low-carbon, and recycling corporations in the economy;
b. prevent environmental and social risks; and
c. improve the performance of environmental and social metrics of banking institutions.

continued on the next page

Box 4 continued

The guidelines cover lending practices to areas including agriculture sectors, rural areas, energy service companies, and firms that provide environmental services and clean energy projects, as well as households willing to retrofit green infrastructure in their homes. For MSMEs, opportunities will arise through the creation of new businesses that will deliver green, low-carbon, and recycling-based products and solutions.

iii. Green Finance Guidelines

More recently in 2022, the PRC issued its third policy called the Green Finance Guidelines, which are designed to provide support to both insurance firms and banking financial institutions. Under these guidelines, environmental and social risks were expanded to include environmental, social, and governance factors. Under this initiative, these guidelines aim to target carbon neutrality in both the portfolios and operations of these entities.

Taken together, these initiatives aim to create financial products which support achieving carbon neutrality. These new financial products include:

i. issuance of green financing instruments linked to reductions in carbon emissions,
ii. green loans which are associated with growing trees whereby the carbon sink acts as collateral in this arrangement,[a]
iii. green loans for the installation of decentralized solar power stations, and
iv. insurance policies for decentralized solar power stations.

Overall, these policies aim to provide benefits to MSMEs in the form of green finance by enabling low-carbon energy initiatives. Other benefits include the provision of green finance of energy-efficient facilities, machines, equipment, vehicles, and key components. MSMEs will benefit from these guidelines as companies seek to pursue carbon targets through the supply chain (via the introduction of scopes 1, 2, and 3 greenhouse gas protocol reporting standards).

[a] A carbon sink is defined as a natural environment or artificial reservoir that absorbs or stores more carbon dioxide from the atmosphere than it releases. Carbon sinks play a vital role in reducing the concentration of greenhouse gases in the atmosphere. Examples of carbon sinks include forests, oceans, wetlands, and specialized agricultural practices.

Source: Authors.

6. Green Finance for MSMEs to Address Food Security

Food systems are a source of environmental damage, including biodiversity loss. For instance, food systems account for about one-third of global emissions (Crippa et al. 2021) and hence need for green finance is urgent and the financial sector must play a major role to catalyze the decarbonization of global agricultural systems. MSMEs are at the heart global food systems and may struggle to make the transition (section 4).

Food systems are also particularly vulnerable to climate-change physical risks, both acute (e.g., wildfires, storms, and flooding) and chronic (e.g., drought, sea level rise) (Shukla et al. 2019). It is very likely that these impacts will fall most heavily on less-developed economies and microenterprises, including rural agricultural producers in those economies leading to decreased food security (Shukla et al. 2019).

Food security is defined by the World Food Summit (FAO 2008) as a state where "all people, at all times, have physical and economic access to sufficient safe and nutritious food that meets their dietary needs and food preferences for an active and healthy life." The four main dimensions of food security include: physical availability of food; economic and physical access to food; food utilization (e.g., the way the human body makes the most of nutrients in the food and the good biological utilization of food consumed); and stability of these three dimensions.[3]

The data collected by the World Bank show the relative severity of food insecurity in the Asia and Pacific region (Figure 11). High insecurity rates are observed in a number of developing economies, while around 10% of populations in some developed economies such as Australia, New Zealand, and the United States are experiencing food insecurity. Further, Figure 12 indicates this issue is worsening in many economies in Asia and the Pacific. Food insecurity and undernourishment are the result of a combination of the abovementioned dimensions, including the food supply–demand imbalance and the affordability of healthy diets as major contributing factors.

On the amount of nutrition intake, it is understood that 465 million people in Asia were undernourished in 2021 (World Food Programme 2023). Further, a report published by the World Health Organization in 2015 indicated that more than 230,000 people a year in the Americas (WHO 2015), Southeast Asia, and Western Pacific regions were dying from foodborne diseases, such as from consuming contaminated food. By death per population, Southeast Asia recorded the second highest rate after the African region. All these statistics indicate the urgency of food security issues in the broader Asia and Pacific region.

[3] World Bank. *What is Food Security.* https://www.worldbank.org/en/topic/agriculture/brief/food-security-update/what-is-food-security.

Figure 11: Food Insecurity in the Population, 2020

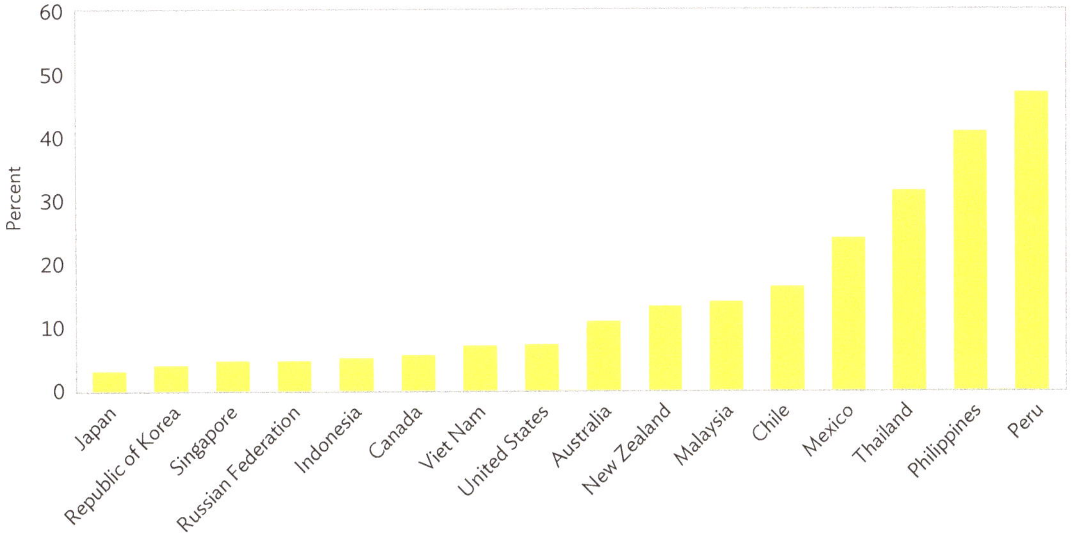

Note: The percentage of people who live in households classified as moderately or severely food insecure. A household is classified as moderately or severely food insecure when at least one adult has reported exposure at times during the year to low-quality diet and reduction in food quantity eaten because of a lack of money or other resources.
Source: Authors based on World Bank. 2023. Prevalence of Moderate or Severe Food Insecurity in the Population (%). https://data.worldbank.org/indicator/SN.ITK.MSFI.ZS.

Figure 12: Change in Food Insecurity in the Population, 2015–2020

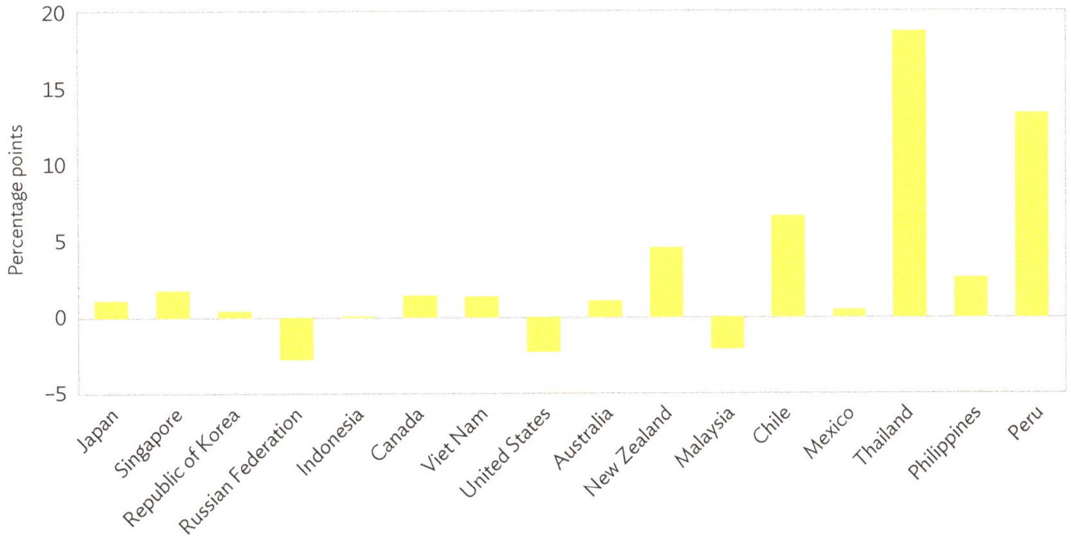

Note: Data for Viet Nam are from 2017 and the Philippines from 2018.
Source: Authors, based on World Bank. 2023. Prevalence of Moderate or Severe Food Insecurity in the Population (%). https://data.worldbank.org/indicator/SN.ITK.MSFI.ZS.

Figure 13: Green Finance Available for the Food Production Sector

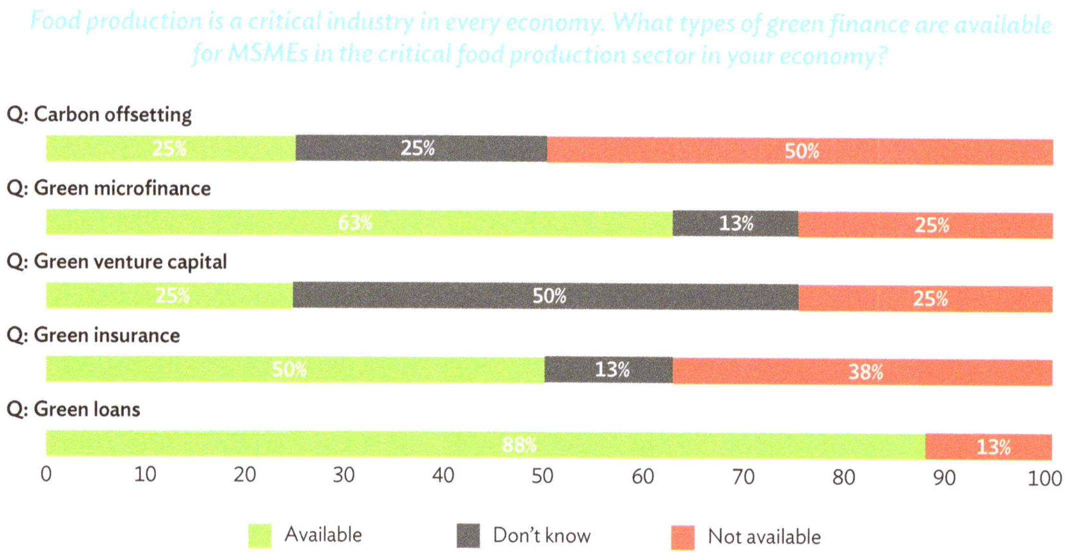

MSMEs = micro, small, and medium-sized enterprises.
Source: ADB Nexus between Green Finance and MSMEs survey result.

The agriculture sector accounts for the largest share of greenhouse gas emissions in Asia and the Pacific (Aryal 2022). The Food and Agriculture Organization of the United Nations (FAO 2022) estimates food losses and waste per capita per year in South and Southeast Asia and in Latin America as approximately 120 to 220 kilograms, and far larger losses and waste come from the production and retail sectors than from the consumers. These facts indicate that improving food security can be viewed as an important component to overcome climate-related issues. Considering the significant contribution MSMEs make to economies in the region,[4] especially with regard to food production and distribution, access to finance can be expected to play an important role in improving food security. For progress to be made on this front, new sources of finance will be vital, as accessing capital markets is often not easy for MSMEs. It would be important to explore if green finance can fill this gap. The survey shows that green capital raising is not always available for MSMEs in the agriculture sector at this stage (Figure 13), while economies that indicated that they don't currently have green finance also acknowledged their need for it. Respondents also acknowledged the important role the microfinance sector can play in supplying green finance to various stakeholder sectors surrounding agricultural businesses (Figure 14). The policy support measures explained in earlier sections and described in the case studies would need to be implemented effectively so that they enhance green finance supply to MSMEs.

[4] According to the Economic and Social Commission for Asia and the Pacific, MSMEs employ an average 69% of the domestic labor forces and 41% of GDP in the Asian economies. https://msmepolicy.unescap.org/overview-msmes-asia-pacific-regions.

Figure 14: Importance of Green Finance to Agriculture-Related Sectors

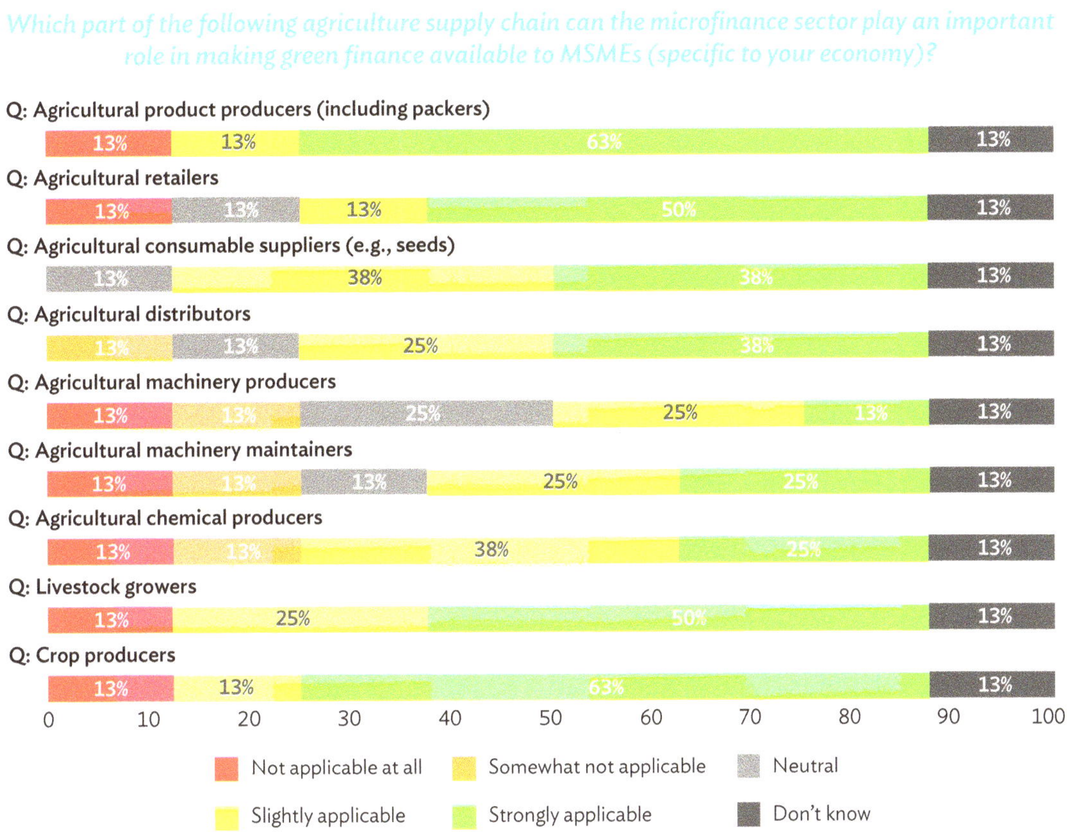

MSMEs = micro, small, and medium-sized enterprises.
Source: ADB Nexus between Green Finance and MSMEs survey result.

7. Enabling MSME Green Finance Through Technology

The rise of new technologies and fintech offers potential to support green finance for MSMEs in emerging economies. New channels between fintech and green finance appear to offer the potential to enable economies to reduce carbon emissions, especially when GDP growth in an economy is driven and dominated by MSMEs (see section 3 and Figure 3).

Studies have shown that fintech can be used to nurture and develop green finance in economies. Nassiry (2018) suggests that fintech can be deployed to enable new green finance technologies such as decentralized electricity markets, carbon credits, and climate finance, including green bonds.

Box 4 presents fintech products and services that could assist MSMEs in gaining access to green financing, including mobile banking, e-wallets, peer-to-peer (P2P) lending, microfinance, sustainable crowdfunding platforms, and education and gamification to digital green finance.

Further, building on the policy discussion in section 5, policymakers play an essential role in promoting green finance by harnessing the potential of fintech in an economy. Fintech can be a powerful tool for advancing green finance policy objectives. Policymakers can promote green finance in many way through fintech, including:

i. **Regulatory sandboxes:** Policymakers can establish innovation hubs to provide a controlled environment for fintech startups to develop and test new green finance solutions. These sandbox environments allow for experimentation while ensuring a specific level of consumer protection and regulatory compliance.

ii. **Licensing and regulatory frameworks:** Government policymakers can introduce specific regulation and licensing for green finance solutions from fintech apps and initiatives. These forms of regulation will assist in meeting green transformation standards while maintaining current stability with present-day infrastructure, processes, and operations of old technology.

iii. **Incentivizing innovation:** Financial incentives can be introduced to encourage the development of fintech solutions that deliver green finance outcomes and benefits. These types of incentives include grants or funding opportunities. Examples of innovative incentives may include platforms for impact investing or carbon offset trading.

iv. **Data sharing and accessibility:** Policymakers can introduce data standards at an economic level, which can encourage data sharing and open application programming interfaces (APIs) that facilitate the integration of ESG-related data into fintech apps and platforms. These standards will facilitate the assessment of environmental risks and opportunities within MSMEs and the economy.

v. **Digital ID and know your customer:** Policymakers can support the development of digital identity solutions that streamline the onboarding process for investors and borrowers, thereby making it easier for both sets of parties to participate in P2P and other green finance initiatives.

Box 5: Fintech Applications

Mobile banking: Mobile banking refers to the use of smartphones or other mobile devices (such as tablets, electronic smart watches, Internet-of-Things appliances, etc.) to complete financial transactions and banking activities. Mobile banking raises accessibility of banking services for more individuals and firms because it enables users to bypass the need to personally visit a physical bank branch to complete transactions. Mobile banking enables the potential of green finance to be delivered to micro, small, and medium-sized enterprises (MSMEs).

E-wallets: An electronic wallet, or digital wallet, is an application or platform that allows individuals or MSMEs to store funds, manage them, and securely conduct electronic financial transactions. E-wallets are designed to replace a physical wallet and provide a convenient and accessible way to make payments, store payment card information, and manage various forms of digital currency. Examples of e-wallets include PayPal, Apple Pay, Google Pay, Venmo, Alipay, WeChat Pay, and Samsung Pay.

P2P lending: Peer-to-peer (P2P) lending, also known as person-to-person lending, is a type of online lending that enables individuals (or "peers") to lend money directly to other individuals or MSMEs without the involvement of intermediaries such as banks or other lending institutions. P2P lending technology apps connect borrowers and lenders via a matching service on an online marketplace. P2P lending creates new benefits specifically for MSMEs as it provides access to credit to those borrowers who may not qualify for traditional bank credit.

Sustainable crowdfunding platforms: Crowdfunding platforms dedicated to green and sustainable projects can attract environmentally conscious investors looking to support MSMEs with a positive environmental impact. These platforms can offer rewards or equity-based crowdfunding options for green initiatives, allowing MSMEs to access capital from a broad pool of like-minded investors.

Education and gamification to digital green finance: Mobile applications can serve as a platform for providing MSMEs with digital education resources on green finance and sustainability best practices. These apps can offer interactive courses, tutorials, and quizzes to improve MSMEs' understanding of green finance and the benefits of eco-friendly initiatives. Through gamification within the apps, the apps can promote reduction energy consumption and reduce waste/carbon footprints/emissions. These scores can lead to potential rewards, or the scores can be seen on a leaderboard for certain competitions.

Source: Authors

vi. **Education and awareness:** Government agencies need to collaborate with fintech firms to develop educational resources and tools to raise awareness about green finance opportunities for MSMEs. These educational programs will encourage individuals and MSMEs to make sustainable business decisions.

vii. **International collaboration:** APEC economies can engage in international cooperation to share best practices, standards, and regulations in relation to green finance and fintech, thereby promoting global consistency and interoperability.

These new technologies and fintech are delivered primarily through public funding and via public–private partnerships as well as the private sector. For example, the Hong Kong Monetary Authority (2021) highlights the current working environment in this space. Policymakers need to figure out how to increase private sector participation in these new technologies rather than relying on continual government support. In other economies, the digital transformation of fintech stems from private sector firms and innovation (BIS 2021).

Studies show that technology can deliver green finance and play a larger role in economies where a large proportion of GDP is generated by MSMEs. For example, Mirza et al. (2023) argue that fintech provides groups with untapped economic potential with access to clean energy, which leads to lower costs, increased efficiency, green savings, and investing in all segments of the broader community. Guang-Wen and Siddik (2023) show that fintech adoption translates to a positive influence on green finance in Bangladesh. Udeagha and Muchapondwa (2023) show that BRICS economies tend to be fossil-fuel intensive, and a shift to green finance products can speed up and promote environmental sustainability in these economies.[5] These recent studies reveal that the development of new technologies and fintech in an economy can enable the following benefits:

- At the macroeconomic level, new technology can be deployed to reduce the carbon intensity of the economy.
- Consumers can be better informed on the sustainability of the good or service they purchase by using technology-based solutions. MSME vendors can use fintech apps to provide more information about their products to consumers. Products that are more green-friendly will attract a higher demand in comparison to conventional products.
- Fintech allows MSMEs to report ESG data on the products they sell as well as potential new reporting standards to government agencies.

Taken together, the increased level of transparency on the sustainability of products and services will allow government agencies to more accurately measure and monitor the levels of green finance being deployed in their respective economies.

Numerous MSMEs have sales and profit margins that are susceptible to seasonality, input and labor costs, late payments, disasters, unexpected expenses, and a multitude of other factors that result in irregular cash flows. Without collateral or adequate credit information, banks are often hesitant to lend them money due to the higher risk of such firms.

Financial institutions are evolving because of fintech, making it easier for MSMEs to obtain loans. Cash-flow-based financing, which is supported by current and projected future cash flows, is gaining popularity (see section 3 discussion of collateral and credit history as a barrier to green finance). These loans are wholly distinct from traditional asset-backed loans, in which the loan amount and term are determined by the collateral offered to the lender. Conventional banks' reluctance to lend to MSMEs stems from the fact that they lack immovable assets as collateral. Fintech opens new avenues for MSMEs to access loans via an app whereby the know-your-customer verification, loan offer, confirmation of acceptance, and the signing of the loan agreement from cash-flow-based financing can be actioned on a mobile app on the same day, with no paperwork and with no geographical barriers within an economy (Arner, Buckley, and Zetzsche 2018; Feyen, Natarajan, and Saal 2023). The impact of fintech will be most effective for MSMEs in island economies in APEC as this new form of delivering financial services will overcome the physical obstacles of geography.

[5] BRICS is an intergovernmental organization comprising Brazil, the People's Republic of China, India, the Russian Federation, and South Africa, and more recently adding Egypt, Ethiopia, Iran, and the United Arab Emirates.

Figure 15: Fintech and Regtech for MSME Green Finance

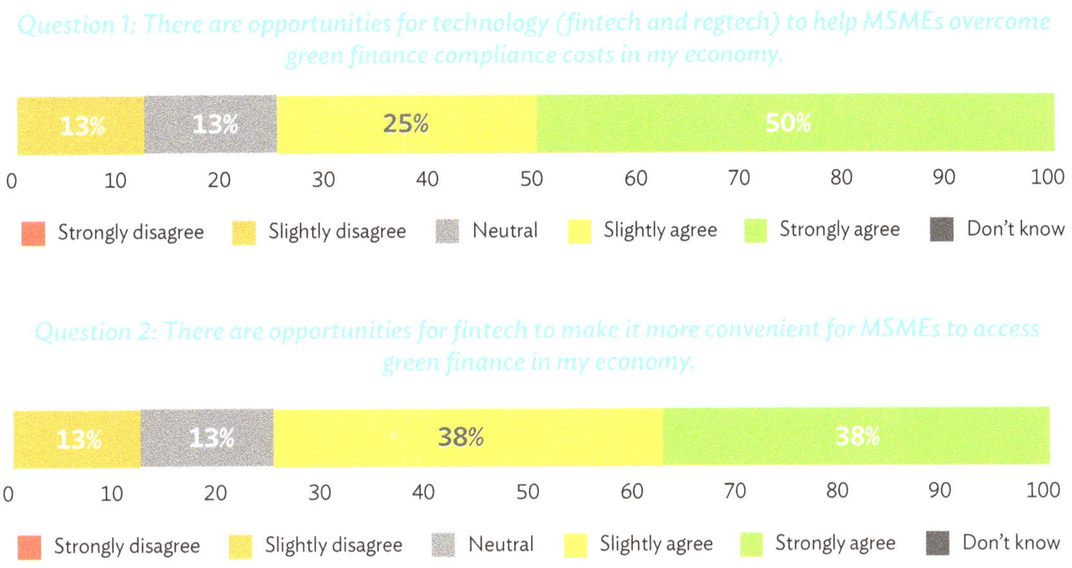

fintech = financial technology; MSME = micro, small, and medium-sized enterprise; regtech = regulatory technology.
Source: ADB Nexus between Green Finance and MSMEs survey result.

The ADB survey explored the current circumstances surrounding fintech and regtech in APEC economies. From Figure 15, it is evident that respondents strongly believe that fintech and regtech can provide opportunities to help MSMEs overcome barriers in relation to accessing green finance (question 1). Furthermore, respondents agree that fintech is a more convenient method to provide opportunities to access green finance for MSMEs (question 2).

New technologies via fintech are available to improve access to green finance for MSMEs (Pellergrino and Abe 2022). These new technologies can speed up and lower costs for MSMEs as they disclose and report on EESG-related metrics to both market participants and policymakers and/or regulators. Apps that allow MSMEs to disclose specific green metrics for different products and services will enable them to digitize and report ESG standards to relevant parties. This type of technology can be used to assist MSMEs in quickening their transformation to lower carbon intensity.

Artificial intelligence (AI), including generative AI (Gen-AI), represents another emerging technology with the potential to enhance both the quantity and quality of green financing for MSMEs. For example, AI can be used to support credit scoring (i.e.,. rapid assessment of non-structured data such as social media), enhance customer support, raise awareness of products or services, or train loan officers. AI can also be used for know-your-customer compliance and cybersecurity. Each of these examples has the potential to significantly lower costs for financial service providers, with savings passed on to customers to make green finance more viable or appealing. However, the effectiveness of AI in green finance hinges on access to high-quality data and the capacity to utilize it effectively, which varies widely across APEC economies.

8. Proposed Actions for Policymakers and Regulators

The rapid expansion of green finance products through better tailoring for the MSME sector, along with the development of processes necessary to improve the level of access to green finance, has great potential to unlock both finance and green development opportunities for enterprises operating within this underserved market. Policymakers and regulators play an important role in achieving this by creating an enabling environment for green financing for MSMEs. The following proposed actions intend to provide guidance to policymakers and regulators on ways to promote green finance opportunities for MSMEs.

Proposed Action 1: Close knowledge gaps.

The provision of green finance products targeting the MSME sector is a relatively new concept in most economies. Knowledge gaps exist about how to improve the supply of green finance by financial institutions and service providers (the supply side) and how to improve awareness and capacity within MSMEs (the demand side). Closing these knowledge gaps requires tailored policy and regulatory reforms to maximize the full potential of green finance for MSMEs. Policymakers can play an important role in addressing the knowledge gaps by:

- Supporting research into green financing and MSMEs via cooperation with relevant research institutions and the private sector to gather data directly from MSMEs, pilot tests of products and services, and disseminate results. These initiatives may include supporting the collection and sharing of case studies that demonstrate effective tools and policies applicable to different types of MSMEs, sectors, and economies.
- Supporting the collection and dissemination of both public and private data that can be used to develop green finance products that address the unique needs of MSMEs.
- Working with stakeholders to define the scope of green finance for MSMEs, taking into account opportunities to expand the scope beyond the adoption of renewable energy or energy-efficient practices (e.g., carbon removal projects that have both nature and climate benefits).
- Developing local and regional economy transition road maps, as well as priority areas for greening MSMEs and how green finance can support these road maps.
- At the regional and global levels, supporting the creation of depositories of knowledge, or toolboxes, to help different economies share their experiences with green finance and MSMEs as they test new initiatives and measure results.
- Recognizing the differing green finance needs and challenges of different MSMEs segments or industries. In particular, attention needs to be given to how green finance can support agricultural MSMEs to augment food security. For instance, agriculture is likely to have greater need for physical risk hazard insurance and adaptation finance than other sectors.

Proposed Action 2: Improve inclusion of MSME aspects into existing and new sustainable finance taxonomies and frameworks.

Several green finance taxonomies and green banking frameworks have been, or are currently being, developed across several economies (see section 2 and Case Study 3). However, the development of these green finance standards is typically done with larger firms in mind and less consideration for MSMEs. Each MSME segment or industry will have unique needs and constraints as they relate to access to finance, as well as unique needs with regard to green finance more specifically. To address this, policymakers should take the following actions:

- Work with industry associations and other key stakeholders to consider how definitions of MSMEs at the local level align with current taxonomies and what challenges may exist for certain MSME segments and industries.
- Include eligible projects and activities specifically for MSMEs as users and suppliers of green technologies and services in green taxonomies (for example, smaller energy efficiency investments [see Case Study 3], circular small-scale farming, etc.).
- Include climate adaptation and mitigation projects as part of the green finance standards, including applicable transition financing.
- Review the applicability and interoperability of taxonomies to meet MSME limitations (e.g., lack of collateral, lack of reporting ability) and specific sector needs (e.g., agribusiness).

Proposed Action 3: Steer financial service providers and MSMEs toward green finance opportunities through incentives and regulatory measures.

Increasing the level of access to green finance requires efforts to steer both the supply of finance and demand from MSMEs to better utilize green finance opportunities (see sections 3 and 5). Policymakers can play an important role in pursuing this by providing incentives and regulatory measures to both financial service providers and MSMEs to accelerate the provision or adoption of green financing. Examples include:

- Introduce or promote incentive schemes that specifically target the expansion of green finance in the MSME sector, for example, through fiscal or monetary measures (e.g., similar to support mechanisms for green bonds where governments provide funding for part of the green verification cost).
- Recognize that changing behaviors through incentive schemes is often a slow process. Thus, policymakers might also consider mandating certain changes where results are needed more urgently, for example, guidance to banks to increase green MSME lending.
- Develop a more direct approach to how government institutions interact with industry, for example, by encouraging state-owned enterprises (including banks) to provide trade financing to MSMEs that meet certain green requirements and including the outcome as part of lending performance criteria. Adopt preferential government purchasing from "green MSMEs" (i.e., green procurement).
- Support the implementation of incentive systems within financial institutions that incentivizes banks to providing green MSME financing, which could be achieved by, for instance, adjusted

risk weighting for climate risk. The Bank for International Settlements (BIS (2022) notes that it is currently developing a suite of supervisory and regulatory measures to address climate-related financial risks. There is also the potential for regulators to lower the risk weighting of green-finance-related assets and loans.

- Consider how existing government subsidy programs, for example, in the agriculture sector, can be tied to measurable indicators of green progress.

Proposed Action 4: Embrace the development and application of fintech and new financial instruments.

Traditional finance systems struggle to serve MSMEs. Fintech can provide opportunities to create new financing channels targeting MSMEs, including those in remote areas and the informal sector, and to digitize and upgrade risk management for financial institutions and service providers (see section 7). Some specific actions policymakers could take to support this initiative may include:

- Develop regulations to improve compatibility and transferability of data, which will facilitate greater cooperation between fintech companies while enabling clients to have more flexibility to choose their preferred providers.
- Utilize digital technology to enable MSMEs to automate data collection and verification relevant to meet key requirements (e.g., on ESG data reporting and audits, or utilize technologies to enable voluntary and/or mandatory carbon reporting).
- Fintech and regtech can also be used to support green finance functions of the financial institutions that serve MSMEs (see Case Study 2).
- Enhance the availability of government funding schemes and support for fintech startups, including incubators, regulatory sandboxes, or pilot programs that support the development of green fintech solutions targeting MSMEs.
- Adopt regulation that facilitates innovative financial instruments to be developed that are relevant to the needs of MSMEs, including products such as microinsurance for climate disasters, biodiversity offsets, or carbon credits.
- Adopt regulatory measures necessary to protect data privacy and address local economy security issues regarding international data transfers and data sharing.

Proposed Action 5: Support capacity development among financial service providers, MSMEs, and other economic actors to adopt green finance.

Dedicated efforts are needed to support the capacity needs of green finance from both supply- and demand-side perspectives. This includes addressing both technical and managerial capabilities among financial service providers and MSMEs. This support may need to be stronger for microfinance institutions which serve microenterprises and are potentially weaker institutionally and more vulnerable to climate shocks (Ahmed et al. 2022). Policymakers can help accelerate the capacity needs of stakeholders through the following:

- Work with relevant industry associations to identify capacity needs and design appropriate interventions for MSMEs.
- Provide regular updates and training (through local government partners or through digital means) to MSMEs on available green financial instruments and support mechanisms, and enhance financial and digital literacy.
- Enable knowledge sharing among MSMEs, and, similarly, among financial institutions, on success cases and experiences of green MSME financing.
- Strengthen knowledge sharing on green technologies and green processes for MSMEs through, for example, roadshows, leaflets, digital means, etc. This can include information on green agriculture technologies, energy efficiency programs, the circular economy, etc.
- Foster cooperation and knowledge sharing among other economic actors (e.g., multinational enterprises) on the advantages and opportunities of green financing for MSMEs.

Proposed Action 6: Develop comprehensive frameworks to leverage technology for expanding green finance access to MSMEs.

Policymakers and regulators should focus on creating an enabling environment that leverages technology to address the unique challenges of green finance for MSMEs. This involves integrating data-driven solutions, AI, and innovation-friendly policies to enhance access, reduce costs, and improve the efficiency of green financing. Key steps include:

- Collaborate with the private sector to create a green data management framework, building on open-banking principles to increase data access and sharing for green finance while ensuring privacy compliance. Policymakers can leverage on the APEC Guiding Principles for Open Data Systems to harmonize and standardize interoperable, scalable, and secure data frameworks across economies.
- Invest in or optimize existing technology infrastructure, such as cloud services, cybersecurity, and blockchain, to support secure and efficient data use for green finance. Promote open API strategies with standardized regulatory frameworks to enable innovative business models, expand green finance access, and improve accountability, while addressing data protection and interoperability.
- Promote AI solutions in green finance for credit scoring, customer support, know-your-customer compliance, and environmental reporting, while ensuring transparency and accountability through clear regulations and pilot programs.
- Establish innovation hubs and provide incentives like tax breaks, green bonds, and regulatory sandboxes to encourage the development and adoption of technology solutions for green finance (ADB 2025).
- Build trust and awareness of green finance technologies through digital financial education programs, integrating climate finance concepts and tailored approaches to meet MSME needs.

References

Ahmed, I., I. Diaz-Rainey, H. Roberts, and D. T. T. Nguyen. 2022. *Expand or Avoid: Microfinance Credit Risk and Climate Vulnerability*. SSRN 4261881.

Alliance for Financial Inclusion (AFI). 2020. *Inclusive Green Finance Policies for MSMEs*. https://www.afi-global.org/sites/default/files/publications/2020-04/AFI_SMEF_IGF%20MSMEs_AW_digital_0.pdf.

________. 2022. *2022 AFI Global Policy Forum Report*. https://www.afi-global.org/wp-content/uploads/2024/10/The-2022-Global-Policy-Forum-GPF-Report_03072023.pdf.

Asia-Pacific Economic Cooperation (APEC). 2007. Sydney APEC Leaders' Declaration on Climate Change, Energy Security and Clean Development. https://www.apec.org/meeting-papers/leaders-declarations/2007/2007_aelm/aelm_climatechange.

________. 2018. *Promoting Innovative Green Financing Mechanisms for Sustainable and Quality Infrastructure Development in the APEC Region*. https://www.apec.org/docs/default-source/publications/2018/9/promoting-green-financing-mechanisms/218_ewg_promoting-green-financing-mechanisms.pdf?sfvrsn=f2672673_1.

________. 2023a. Sustainable Development. https://www.apec.org/groups/other-groups/sustainable-development.

________. 2023b. Energy. https://www.apec.org/groups/som-steering-committee-on-economic-and-technical-cooperation/working-groups/energy.

________. 2023c. Finance Ministers' Process. https://www.apec.org/groups/other-groups/finance-ministers-process.

________. 2023d. *APEC Green Finance Report – Unlocking the Urban Energy Transition*. https://www.apec.org/publications/2023/03/apec-green-finance-report-unlocking-the-urban-energy-transition.

Asia-Pacific Financial Inclusion Forum (APFIF). 2023. APEC Asia-Pacific Financial Inclusion: Policy Approaches to Support Green Financing of Micro, Small, and Medium-sized Enterprises.

Asian Development Bank (ADB). 2021. *Asian Development Outlook 2021: Financing a Green and Inclusive Recovery*.

________. 2025. *Asia Small and Medium-sized Enterprise Monitor 2025: Global Uncertainty, Trade, and Private Sector Businesses in Asia and the Pacific*.

Arner, D.W., R.P. Buckley, and D.A. Zetzsche. 2018. Fintech for Financial Inclusion: A Framework for Digital Financial Transformation. *University of New South Wales Law Research Series*. 87. Sydney.

Aryal, J. P. 2022. Contribution of Agriculture to Climate Change and Low-Emission Agricultural Development in Asia and the Pacific. *ADBI Working Paper Series. No. 1340*. ADB Institute. https://www.adb.org/sites/default/files/publication/829581/adbi-wp1340.pdf.

Association of Southeast Asian Nations (ASEAN). 2023. Taxonomy for Sustainable Finance. https://asean.org/book/asean-taxonomy-for-sustainable-finance/.

Bakken, R. 2021. What Is Sustainable Finance and Why Is It Important? Blog. Harvard Extension School. 9 August. https://extension.harvard.edu/blog/what-is-sustainable-finance-and-why-is-it-important/.

Bank for International Settlements (BIS). 2022. Basel Committee Advances Work on Evaluating Basel III Reforms and Addressing Climate-Related Financial Risks, and Approves Annual G-SIB Assessment. Press release. 15 September.

Beck, S., K. Kim, A. Pandey, M. Tayag, M. Latoja, and A. Malaket. 2023. 2023 Trade Finance Gaps, Growth, and Job Survey. *ADB Briefs*. No. 256. ADB. https://www.adb.org/sites/default/files/publication/906596/adb-brief-256-2023-trade-finance-gaps-growth-jobs-survey.pdf.

Bihari, S. and B. Pandey. 2015. Green Banking in India. *Journal of Economics and International Finance*. 7 (1): pp. 1–17.

Brown, M., B. Guin, and K. Kirschemann. 2016. Microfinance Banks and Financial Inclusion. *Review of Finance*. 20 (3): pp. 907–946.

Burns, A. 2022, New Study Shows Barriers to Financing for MSMEs in Developing and Emerging Countries. *Finance Watch*. https://www.finance-watch.org/press-release/new-study-shows-barriers-to-financing-for-msmes-in-developing-and-emerging-countries/.

Cheok, D. and S. K. Singh. 2018. Identifying Green, Sustainable and Innovative MSMEs in APEC. *APEC Policy Support Unit. Policy Brief No. 19.*

Collins, D. and A. Junghans. 2015. Sustainable Facilities Management and Green Leasing: The Company Strategic Approach. *Procedia Economics and Finance*. 21: pp. 128–136.

Crippa, M., E. Solazzo, D. Guizzardi, F. Monforti-Ferrario, F. N. Tubiello, and A. J. N. F. Leip. 2021. Food Systems Are Responsible for a Third of Global Anthropogenic GHG Emissions. *Nature Food*. 2 (3): pp. 198–209.

Dembele, F., R. Schwarz, and P. Horrocks. 2021. *Scaling Up Green, Social, Sustainability and Sustainability-Linked Bond Issuances in Developing Countries*. OECD Publishing.

Dorfleitner, G., Q. Nguyen, and M. Rohe. 2019, Microfinance Institutions and the Provision of Mobile Financial Services: First Empirical Evidence. *Finance Research Letters*. 31: pp. 357–362.

Elie, L., C. Granier, and S. Rigot. 2021. The Different Types of Renewable Energy Finance: A Bibliometric Analysis. *Energy Economics*. 93: 104997.

European Commission. 2023. EU Taxonomy Navigator. Brussels. https://ec.europa.eu/sustainable-finance-taxonomy/.

Feyen, E., J. Frost, L. Gambacorta, H. Natarajan, and M. Saal. 2021. Fintech and the digital transformation of financial services: implications for market structure and public policy. *BIS Papers*. No. 117. Bank for International Settlements and the World Bank Group. https://www.bis.org/publ/bppdf/bispap117.pdf.

Feyen, E., H. Natarajan, and M. Saal. 2023. *Fintech and the Future of Finance: Market and Policy Implications*. World Bank.

Fleming, S. 2020. What is Green Finance and Why Is It Important? World Economic Forum. https://www.weforum.org/agenda/2020/11/what-is-green-finance/.

Food and Agriculture Organization (FAO). 2008. An Introduction to the Basic Concepts of Food Security. FAO Food Security Programme.

________. 2022. *Global Food Losses and Food Waste: Extent, Cause and Prevention*. https://www.fao.org/3/mb060e/mb060e.pdf.

Gifford, R. 2018. *Accelerating Green Finance.* A Report to Government by the Green Finance Taskforce.

Greitens, J. 2023. Sustainable Finance and Small and Medium Enterprises. *Intereconomics.* 58 (4): pp. 222–226.

Guang-Wen, Z. and A. B. Siddik. 2023. The Effect of Fintech Adoption On Green Finance And Environmental Performance Of Banking Institutions during the COVID-19 Pandemic: The Role of Green Innovation. *Environmental Science and Pollution Research.* 30: 25959–25971.

Hendrichs, H. and T. Busch. 2012. Carbon Management as a Strategic Challenge for SMEs. *Greenhouse Gas Measurement and Management*. 2 (1): pp. 61–72.

Hong Kong Monetary Authority. 2021. *A Vision For Technology-Driven Green Finance*. Project Genesis – Report 1. BIS Innovation Hub, Hong Kong Centre.

Hu, Y., S. Du, Y. Wang, and X. Yang. 2023. How Does Green Insurance Affect Green Innovation? Evidence from China. *Sustainability*. 15 (16): p. 12194.

ICG Consulting Canada Inc. 2007. *Green Financial Products and Services: Current Trends and Future Opportunities in North America.* Report of the North Task Force (NATF) of the United Nations Environment Program Finance Initiative.

Inclusive Finance Working Group (IGFWG). 2022. Roadmap for Inclusive Green Finance Implementation.

Katris, A. and K. Turner. 2021. Can Different Approaches to Funding Household Energy Efficiency Deliver on Economic and Social Policy Objectives? ECO and Alternatives in the UK. *Energy Policy*. 155: p. 112375.

Lamptey, R. and M. Ngoasong. 2023. The Role of Governance in Enabling the Pursuit of Dual Mission in Based-Based Impact Investing. *Entrepreneurship and Regional Development*. 35 (3–4): pp. 382–401.

Lee, W. Y. and D. Fung. 2023. Current Deficiencies and Reinforcement of Institutional Pillars for Reform in the Green Insurance Market: A Systematic Review. *European Journal of Sustainable Development Research*. 7 (4). Article No: em0235.

Mirza, N., M. Umar, A. Afzal, and S.F. Firdousi. 2023. The Role of Fintech in Promoting Green Finance, And Profitability: Evidence from the Banking Sector in the Euro Zone. *Economic Analysis and Policy*. 78: pp. 33–40.

Nassiry, D. 2018. The Role of Fintech in Unlocking Green Finance: Policy Insights for Developing Countries. *ADBI Working Paper* 883. Asian Development Bank Institute. https://www.adb.org/publications/role-fintech-unlocking-green-finance.

Nguyen, Q., I. Diaz-Rainey, A. Kitto, B. McNeil, N. Pittman, and R. Zhang. 2023. Scope 3 Emissions: Data Quality and Machine Learning Prediction Accuracy. *USAEE Working Paper* No. 22-562. https://ssrn.com/abstract=4191648.

Nguyen, Q., I. Diaz-Rainey, D. Kuruppuarachchi. 2021. Predicting Corporate Carbon Footprints for Climate Finance Risk Analyses–A Machine Learning Approach. *Energy Economics*. 95: p. 10529.

Nie, P. and Z. Li. 2017. Green Insurance Subsidy for Promoting Clean Production Innovation. *Journal of Cleaner Production*. 148 (1): pp. 111–117.

Organisation for Economic Co-operation and Development (OECD). 2022. Financing SMEs for Sustainability Drivers, Constraints and Policies. *OECD SME and Entrepreneurship Papers*.

_______. 2023. Green Finance and Investment. https://www.oecd-ilibrary.org/environment/green-finance-and-investment_24090344.

Painuly, J. and N. Wohlgemuth. 2006. Renewable Energy Financing: What Can We Learn from Experience in Developing Countries? *Energy Studies Review*. 14 (2): pp. 154–170.

Pellergrino, A. and M. Abe. 2022. Digital Financing for SMEs' Recovery in the Post-COVID Era: A Bibliometric Review. *Frontiers in Sustainable Cities*. 4.

Shukla, P. R., J. Skea, E. Calvo Buendia, V. Masson-Delmotte, H. O. Pörtner, D. C. Roberts, and J. Malley, eds. 2019. *Climate Change and Land: An IPCC Special Report on Climate Change, Desertification, Land Degradation, Sustainable Land Management, Food Security, and Greenhouse Gas Fluxes In Terrestrial Ecosystems*. Intergovernmental Panel on Climate Change. https://www.ipcc.ch/site/assets/uploads/2019/11/SRCCL-Full-Report-Compiled-191128.pdf.

Taskforce on Climate-related Financial Disclosures. 2022. *Status Report*. https://assets.bbhub.io/company/sites/60/2022/10/2022-TCFD-Status-Report.pdf.

Udeagha, M. C. and E. Muchapondwa. 2023. Green Finance, Fintech, and Environmental Sustainability: Fresh Policy Insights from the BRICS Nations. *International Journal of Sustainable Development and World Ecology*.

Um, W. 2023. A Regional Asian Green Standard Would Help Unlock Trillions. *Nikkei Asia*. 11 September. https://asia.nikkei.com/Opinion/A-regional-Asian-green-standard-would-help-unlock-trillions.

United Nations Environment Programme (UNEP). 2016. Definition and Concepts. Nairobi. https://unepinquiry.org/wp-content/uploads/2016/09/1_Definitions_and_Concepts.pdf.

_______. 2016. Inquiry: Design of a Sustainable Financial System.

World Food Programme. 2023. The Global Food Crisis: Impact on the Asia Pacific Region. https://www.wfp.org/publications/global-food-crisis-impact-asia-pacific-region.

World Health Organization (WHO). 2015. WHO's First Ever Global Estimates of Foodborne Diseases Find Children Under 5 Account for Almost One Third of Deaths. News release. 3 December. https://www.who.int/news/item/03-12-2015-who-s-first-ever-global-estimates-of-foodborne-diseases-findchildren-under-5-account-for-almost-one-third-of-deaths.

www.ingramcontent.com/pod-product-compliance
Lightning Source LLC
Chambersburg PA
CBHW041800220926
51847CB00014B/265
* 9 7 8 9 2 9 2 7 7 5 7 9 7 *